HIDDEN HISTORY *of* STATEN ISLAND

HIDDEN HISTORY *of* STATEN ISLAND

Theresa Anarumo & Maureen Seaberg

THE History PRESS

Published by The History Press
Charleston, SC
www.historypress.net

First published 2017

Manufactured in the United States

ISBN 9781467138680

Library of Congress Control Number: 2017953984

To the original captain crash, and my angels Stefanie, Joe and Nick…my moving buddies, my best friends, my inspirations—thank you all for the endless love and support.

To Maureen, my dear friend and collaborator, thank you for embarking on this journey with me celebrating our hometown.

Xo
Theresa

****

To my family and friends and wider community on Staten Island—the best is yet to come!

To my lovely high school friend and coauthor Theresa and the great people at The History Press, thank you for making me part of this journey.

Maureen

Contents

Acknowledgements

Hidden History of Staten Island would not have been possible if it were not for the passionate efforts of Staten Island historians, museum curators and community leaders. Their dedication to the preservation of Staten Island's history is greatly admired, respected and sincerely appreciated.

Special thanks to Gabriella Leone, gatekeeper of the Staten Island Archives; Rachel Somma of the Staten Island Museum; Meredith Sladek of Snug Harbor Cultural Center and Botanical Garden; and Celestina Cuadrado of the National Lighthouse Museum, as well as landmark tour guides for your infinite wisdom, graciousness and enthusiasm in this project.

Lastly, a special thank-you to our editor J. Banks Smither for his guidance and support and thanks to the amazing team at The History Press.

Introduction

With more than $1 billion being invested in Staten Island's waterfront from St. George to Stapleton and many other major upgrades in retail and other services around the borough, Richmond County is finally poised to reach its potential as a world-class New York City destination for new residents and visitors alike.

Staten Island may be the least familiar of Gotham's boroughs, but it has a history as rich as any part of the city. It has been home to many literary, revolutionary and pop culture heroes for centuries. This history hasn't really been "hidden," as journalists living here have long been documenting these treasures, but because Staten Island is often overshadowed by more populous and media-filled corners of the city, these legacies are still not widely known.

As the greenest frontier of New York City, the Island is also increasingly diverse, with major diasporas from Liberia and Sri Lanka and other points around the globe. It is still the most Italian-American congressional district in the nation, and you can find a gourmet meal from any of Italy's regions here or take part in that vibrant culture in any one of several arts centers.

Did you know that after working with the king's children in the Court of Siam, governess Anna Leonowens came here to write about it and run a school for children? Or that author George R.R. Martin based "Westeros"—now immortalized in *Game of Thrones*—on his memories of looking out on Staten Island from his boyhood home in Bayonne, New Jersey? Or that chewing gum was invented here with the help of Mexican general Antonio Lopez de Santa Anna? How about country music legend Roy Clark getting his start as a virtuoso guitar player on the Staten Island Ferry? Or that O.J. Simpson prosecutor Marcia Clark graduated from Susan Wagner High School here? How about President Donald Trump doing his real estate apprenticeship here at the many buildings his father, Fred, used to own?

These are just a few of the many stories you'll find within this volume, which is a valentine by former high school classmates and friends to not only longtime residents of the place the Wu-Tang Clan likes to call "Shaolin" but all the many new people who will move to Staten Island or visit here for the first time. Welcome to "The Rock," as the locals like to call it. We hope you enjoy these vignettes and succeed to contribute new legacies of your own making.

Chapter 1

The Guiding Lights of Staten Island

The National Lighthouse Museum

From St. George through Stapleton, Staten Island is transforming into a tourism, retail and residential hub with more than $1 billion in private and public investment. One of the highlights of this long-awaited renaissance is the National Lighthouse Museum, located on the former site of the United States Lighthouse Service's (USLHS) General Depot in St. George, Staten Island. The National Lighthouse Museum educates visitors about the history and technology of the nation's lighthouses. It is a private, nonprofit museum and opened in August 2015.

"The General Depot was the national headquarters, testing ground and distribution center for all materials and equipment used by light keepers and USLHS personnel from 1864 to 1939. Once a lively and bustling site of eighteen buildings, only seven survive today," explains Celestina Cuadrado, the curator and site manager. "The museum is currently housed in the 1912 foundry building and is self-guided. Exhibits include Nantucket to New Jersey: Navigating New York Harbor; Optics: Projecting the Light; and Life at the Light: Lighthouse Keepers. The museum also offers public programs and seasonal lighthouse boat tours."

The historic General Depot site is now being transformed into Lighthouse Point, a commercial and residential development adjacent to the museum in St. George near the Staten Island Ferry. Two glass high-rise buildings and the restoration of the five remaining General

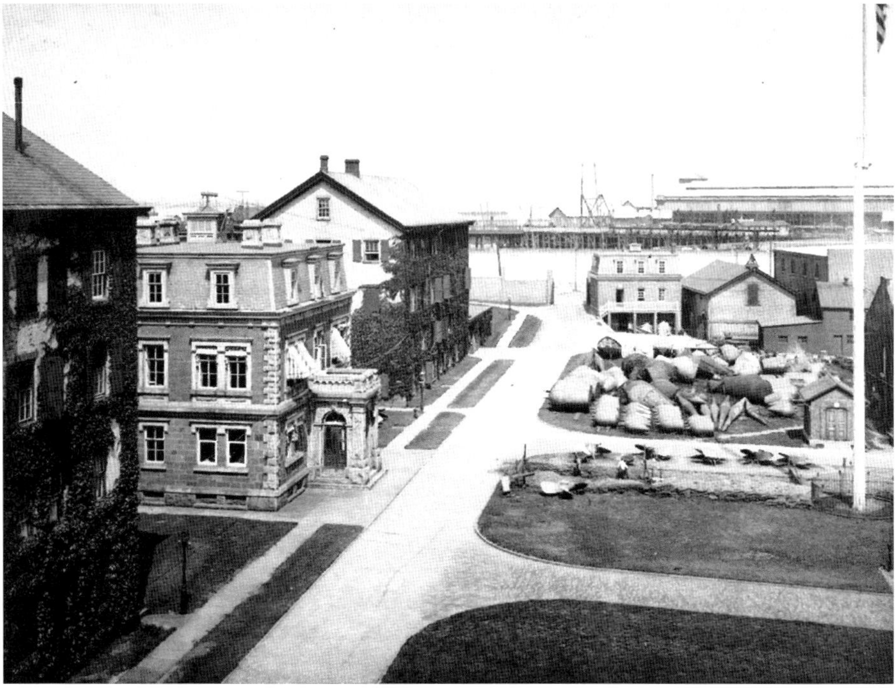

Overview of General Depot Site, circa 1890. *Courtesy National Lighthouse Museum.*

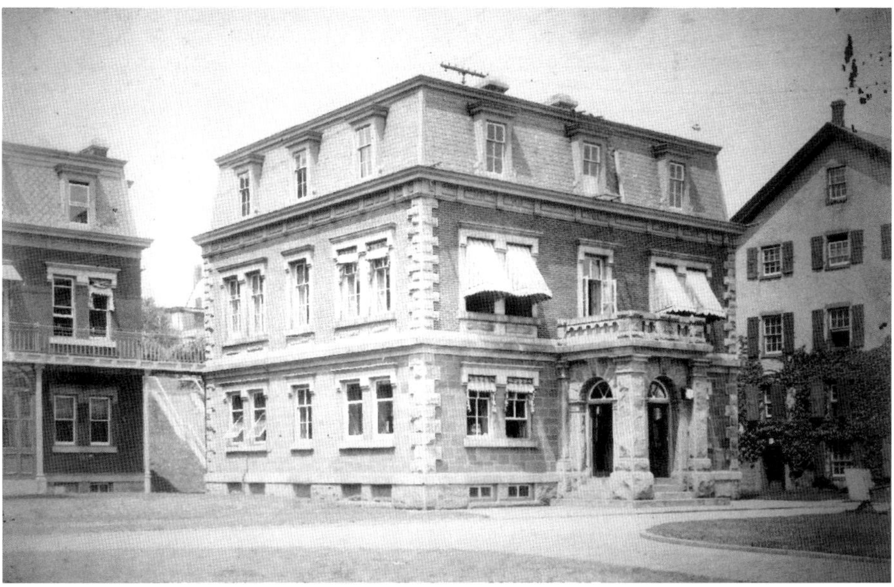

View of Administration Building, circa 1910. *Courtesy National Lighthouse Museum.*

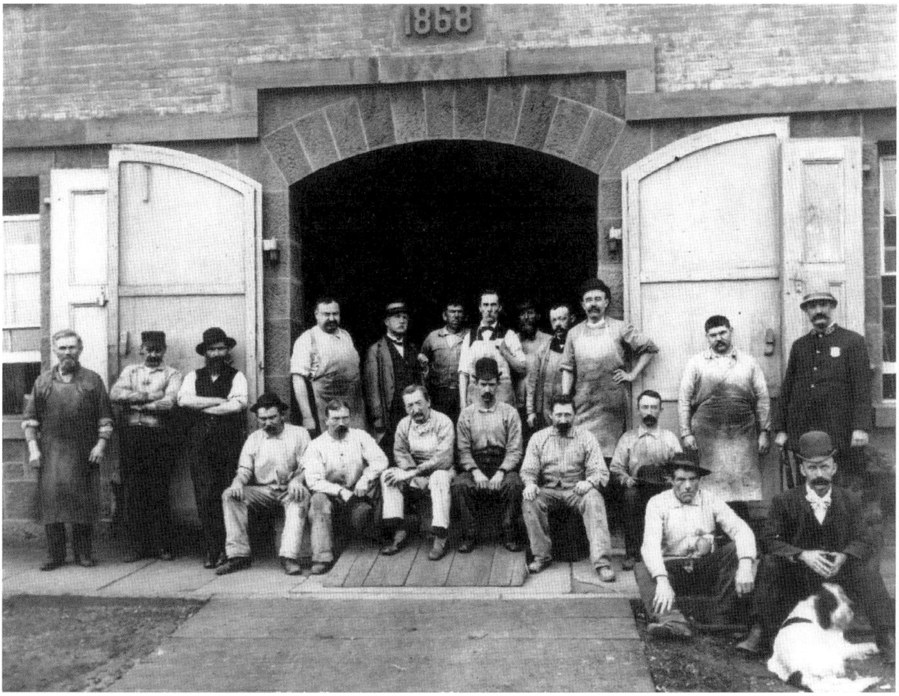

Workers outside Original Lamp Shop, 1890. *Courtesy National Lighthouse Museum.*

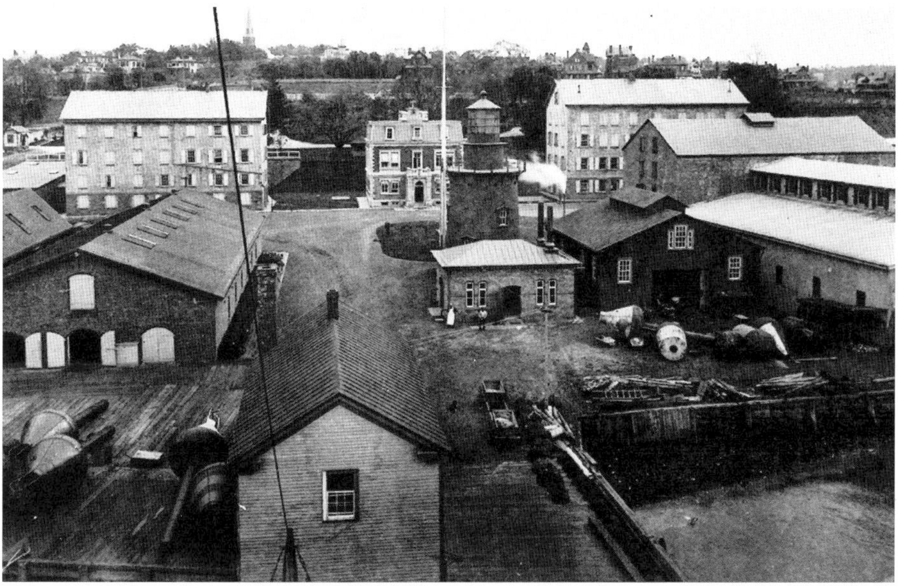

Overview of General Depot Site with experimental lighthouse, circa 1890. *Courtesy National Lighthouse Museum.*

Depot buildings are slated to be completed in the next few years. This will complement the opening of the New York Wheel in 2018, the largest observational wheel in the western hemisphere, and Empire Outlets, the only outlet mall in New York City.

Chapter 2

What's in a Name?

Staten Island is a mass of land encompassing fifty-eight square miles and, according to *State & County QuickFacts—Richmond County* (2016 United Census Bureau), is home to over 470,000 residents. It is the least populated of all the boroughs and the third largest in size. Ideally located in proximity to New York and New Jersey, residents have the opportunity to use the Staten Island Ferry or the Verrazano Bridge to travel into Manhattan, or they can use the Outerbridge Crossing, the Goethals Bridge and the Bayonne Bridge to visit New Jersey.

Staten Island's early history dates back to the late 1500s, when its first inhabitants were Native Americans. In *The Anthropological Papers of the American Museum of Natural History* (Vols. 3–4) by the American Museum of Natural History, artifacts also document an unmarked Native American burial ground located on the grounds of the Conference House Park.

As european settlement began in the 1600s, Henry Hudson, the English explorer, was commissioned to sail for the Dutch Republic. As cited in Russell Shorto's *The Island at the Center of the World: The Epic Story of Dutch Manhattan and the Forgotten Colony that Shaped America*, Henry Hudson sailed his ship, *Half Moon*, into the Bay of New York; upon landing on the Island, the Dutch named it Staaten Eylandt. An old myth regarding the name is a joke that states when excited Dutch explorers saw Staten Island, they enthusiastically exclaimed, "Is dat an island?"

As written by Gajus Scheltema and Heleen Westerhuijs in *Exploring Historic Dutch New York*, the capital of the New Netherland colony was Manhattan;

however, Dutch settlement on Staten Island had not yet occurred due to the many conflicts with the local Native American tribes living there. By 1661, Dutch settlements on Staten Island began to exist and comprised a small group of Dutch and French Huguenot families, as told in Edward Robb Ellis's *The Epic of New York City*. Today, there are many town names on present-day Staten Island that are rooted in their Dutch history, such as Huguenot, New Dorp and Old Town, to name just a few.

In Sewell Chan's 2007 *New York Times* article "That Old Tale about S.I.? Hold on Now," he references how the Native Americans ceded their claim to the land of Staten Island to the English, and shortly thereafter, at the end of the Second Anglo-Dutch War in 1667, the Treaty of Breda was agreed upon, relieving the Dutch of all their parcels of the New Netherlands land. Further mentioned in *The Anthropological Papers of the American Museum of Natural History* (Vols. 3–4), it states the English established colonies, which were then divided into counties, and Staaten Eylandt was renamed Richmond County after the first duke of Richmond. According to Evarts B. Greene and Virginia D. Harrington's *American Population before the Federal Census of 1790*, the English divided Staten Island into four quadrants of property, giving English naval captains, governors and lords ample parcels of the most desirable land based on its natural features such as proximity along waterways, fertile hills and vibrant coastal areas.

As a result of having such lush land that is rich in soil and robust coastlines, Staten Island was full of bountiful opportunity. Its unchartered and unexplored fields and its majestic hills would define Staten Island as a cornerstone for some of the most prestigious neighborhoods, beaches, communities and businesses in the twentieth century.

According to the New York Public Library's "New York City: Staten Island on the Web," and as mentioned in *Encyclopedia Britannica Eleventh Edition*, from the late 1700s, Staten Island was largely known as Richmond County/the Borough of Richmond. However, as cited by Jeffrey A. Kroessler in *New York, Year by Year: A Chronology of the Great Metropolis*, in the year 1975, the Borough of Richmond became the Borough of Staten Island.

Moreover, if you're a fan of hip-hop music and pop culture, you may be familiar with the word "Shaolin," as it has become yet another trendy name referring to the Borough of Staten Island. This nickname was made popular by the internationally acclaimed rap group the Wu-Tang Clan. These former Staten Island residents mention their youthful days in the borough, affectionately calling it "Shaolin" in their rhythmic rap lyrics.

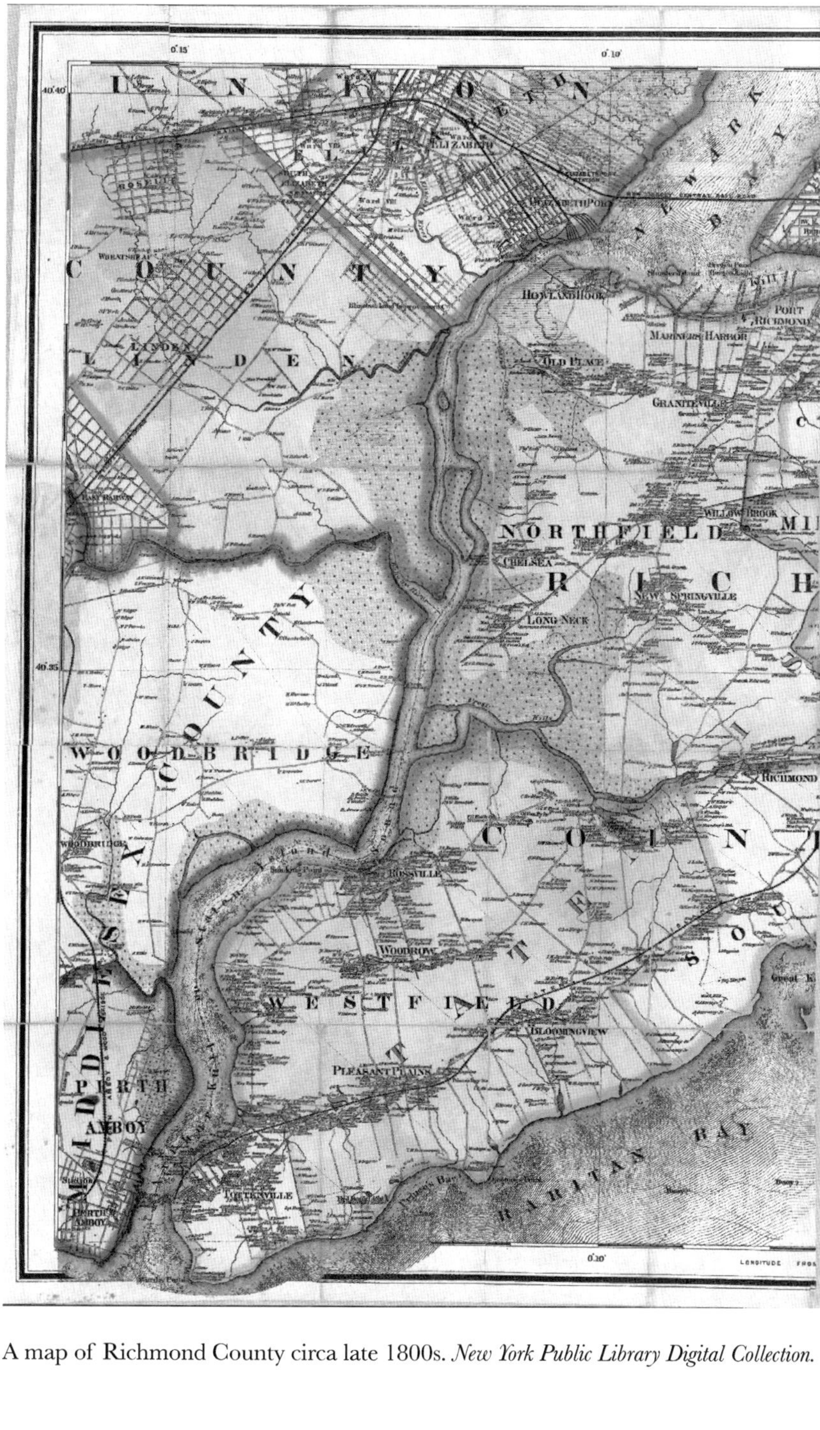

A map of Richmond County circa late 1800s. *New York Public Library Digital Collection.*

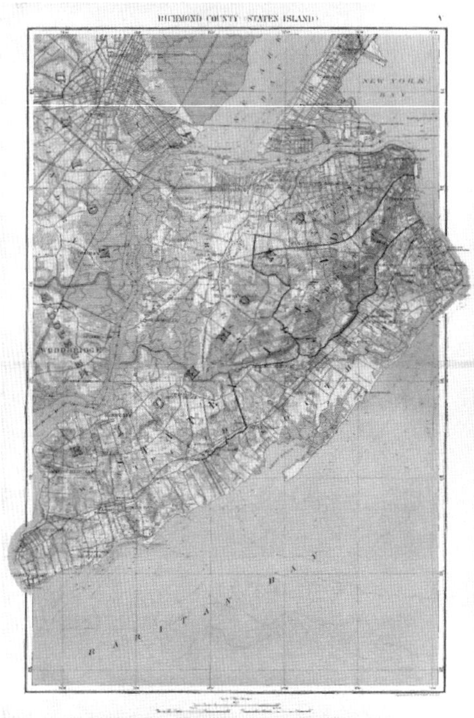

Left: A map of Richmond County, showing its topography and streets, circa late 1800s. *Wikimedia Commons.*

Below: A map of Richmond County with views of its borders, circa late 1800s. *New York Public Library Digital Collection.*

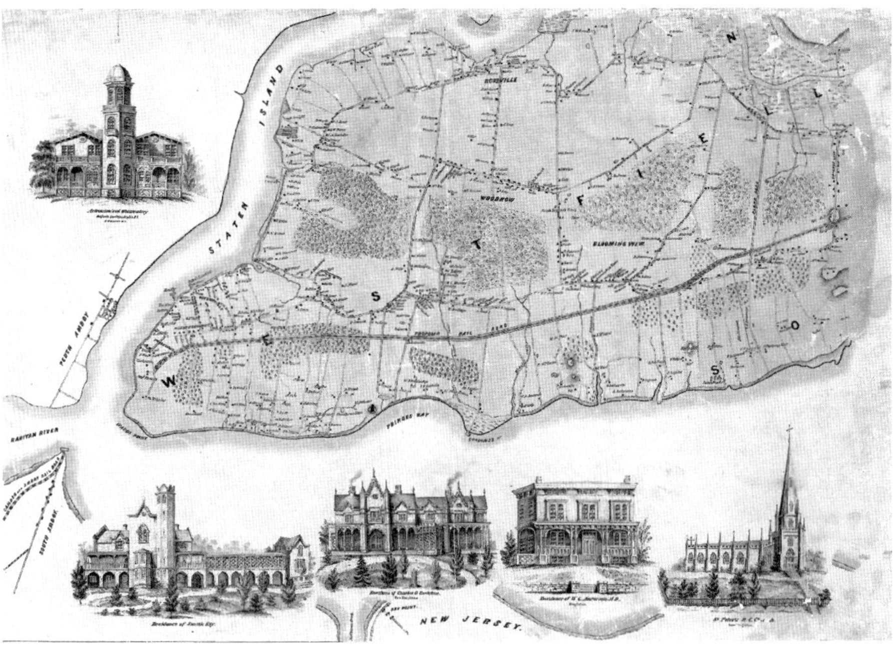

Today, Staten Island is most often referred to as the "Forgotten Borough," a reference to it being overshadowed by the other New York City boroughs. As noted in Cara Buckley's 2007 article "Bohemia by the Bay" and Chip Brown's 1994 article "Escape from New York," both from the *New York Times*, this moniker stems from the perception that the Island may not be considered as hip and cool when compared to other New York City boroughs, or perhaps how some residents believe their needs can be overlooked by city governmental officials. Moreover, Staten Island is the only borough that is not connected to the NYC subway system, furthering the argument of a disconnection from New York City.

Staten Island is an outdoorsman's delight, warranting yet another popular nickname, the "Greenest Borough." Home to 170 grandiose parks sprinkled across twelve thousand acres, parks such as Clove Lakes Park, Silver Lake Park, the Staten Island Greenbelt, High Rock Park, Great Kills Park, Wolfe's Pond Park, Mount Loretto Park and the Conference House Park are full of hiking and biking trails, ponds and nature observation points. Some parks have access to the harbor for fishing and boating, and most offer festivals, outdoor events and opportunities for athletics. There is also the 2.5-mile Franklin D. Roosevelt Boardwalk that runs adjacent to the beaches, where residents and visitors alike enjoy biking and walking opportunities. Many choose to live on this beautiful island and find it offers a taste of suburbia right outside the hustle-bustle of New York City.

With the Staten Island renaissance well underway, $1.5 billion has been invested in development of the St. George and Stapleton neighborhoods. The area will provide residents and surrounding communities the world's largest Ferris wheel, an abundance of waterfront luxury apartments, fine restaurants, a plethora of entertainment and the Empire Shopping Outlets.

Chapter 3

Snug Harbor Cultural Center and Botanical Garden

Snug Harbor Cultural Center and Botanical Garden is one of Staten Island's most historical and architectural gems. Encapsulated by a landmarked nineteenth-century wrought-iron fence, Snug Harbor is nestled on beautifully landscaped grounds encompassing over eighty acres and located on the New Brighton waterfront, minutes from the Staten Island Ferry.

It is a nonprofit organization dedicated to offering dynamic programming in arts, education, horticulture and recreation to Staten Island and its surrounding communities; its museums play a vital role in the preservation of Staten Island's history.

Sailors' Snug Harbor: The Early Years

Upon his death in 1801, Captain Robert Richard Randall bequeathed his rural twenty-four-acre estate in Manhattan (present-day Greenwich Village) to house Sailors' Snug Harbor, a retirement home intended for sea-worn sailors. According to Gerald J. Barry's *The Sailors' Snug Harbor: A History, 1801–2001*, Randall's will specified that Snug Harbor would be for "maintaining aged, decrepit, and worn-out sailors." This charity, founded by Randall, was to become one of the first charitable institutions in the United States. However, family members contested his will, and this legal dilemma delayed the project for many years. By the time the conflict was resolved in Randall's favor, the Manhattan property had increased in value to become prime real estate. His board of trustees decided that in lieu of building Snug Harbor there, they would subdivide the Manhattan property and lease its row houses. As a result of the shrewd business decisions made by the harbor trustees, profits from the Manhattan long-term leases enabled the purchase of 160 acres along the North Shore of Staten Island, providing the construction and maintenance of Sailors' Snug Harbor.

ARCHITECTURE AND DESIGN

In 1833, Sailors' Snug Harbor, a haven for seafarers, opened; it was designed as a lavish, self-sustained community for retired mariners. Many of these men were penniless and found refuge in the new home that awaited them onshore, as referenced at www.noblemaritime.org/sailors-snug-harbor.

The center building, positioned in a line of five classic temple-like massive structures, is known as Building C, and it set the highest standard for those flanking it to follow. Designed by Minard Lafever in the Greek Revival style, its grandiose stature is captivating. Its monumental portico, designed with eight columns, commands attention and leaves you in awe. Two similar buildings were built on each of its sides with the same splendor, facing the front lawn. The "Front Five," as they are commonly known, interlock by smaller connecting structures set behind their grand façades, as described by David Dunlap in his 2008 *New York Times* article "Dispute Grows." The five waterfront buildings are the pillars of Sailors' Snug Harbor's foundation and a testament to its nineteenth-century history. Iconic and resounding, they represent the town-like community that once was, set against a backdrop of laurel trees and pastures.

The lawns were outlined with chestnut trees, pine trees, gardens and gazebos. There were ponds, lakes and an opulent fountain that complemented the illustrious estate; a bronze statue of Robert Randall by artist Augustus Saint-Gaudens was erected in honor of its founder.

In addition to the "Front Five" (which were the main hall and dormitories), and in contrast in scale and design to the Greek Revival buildings, a small Italianate chapel was built, and adjacent to it, a replica of a London cathedral was erected. A tremendous residence for Snug Harbor's governor and a line of cottages for the extensive staff graced the tranquil grounds. Furthermore, a greenhouse, a hospital, a morgue, a pier and a bathhouse on the Kill Van Kull waterway were present. Originally

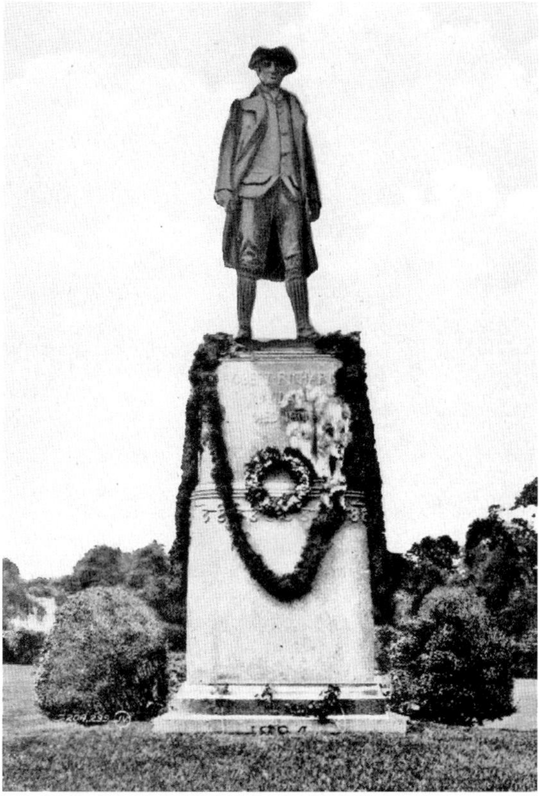

Left: The Robert Richard Randall Statue, designed by artist Augustus Saint-Gaudens. The statue was erected in honor of Randall, founder of Sailors' Snug Harbor, Staten Island. *New York Public Library Digital Collection.*

Below: Building A, which is part of the "Front Five" majestic structures in Sailors' Snug Harbor, is also a former dormitory building used by the sailors. It is a National Historic Landmark today. *New York Public Library Digital Collection.*

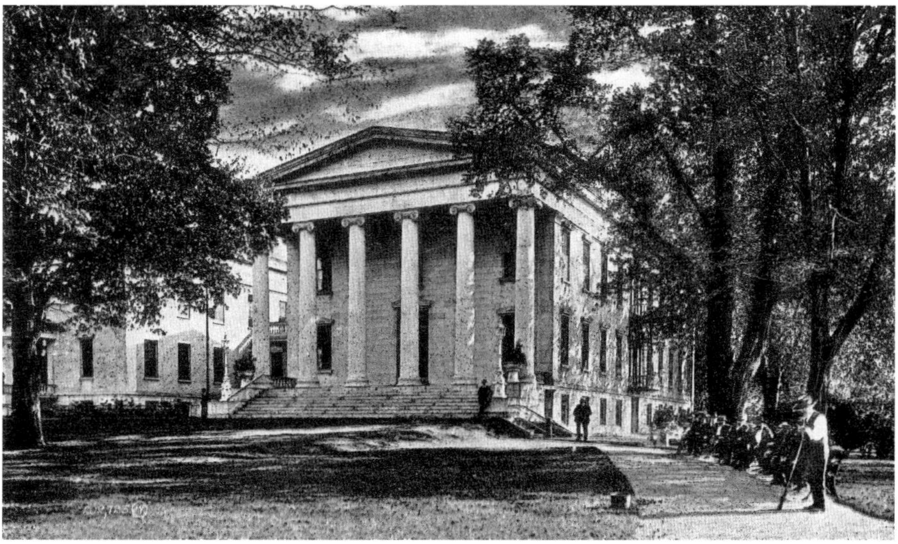

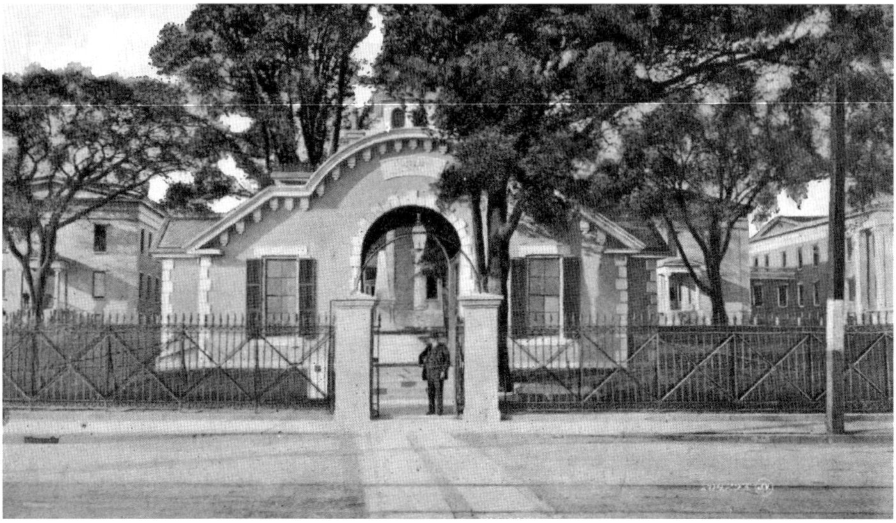

The entrance gates to Sailors' Snug Harbor, Staten Island. *New York Public Library Digital Collection*.

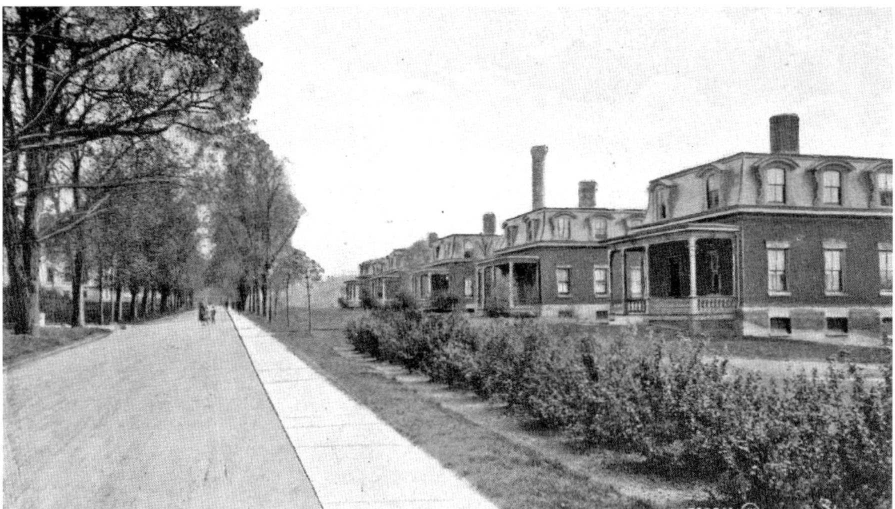

A view of the staff cottages on the Sailors' Snug Harbor grounds. *New York Public Library Digital Collection.*

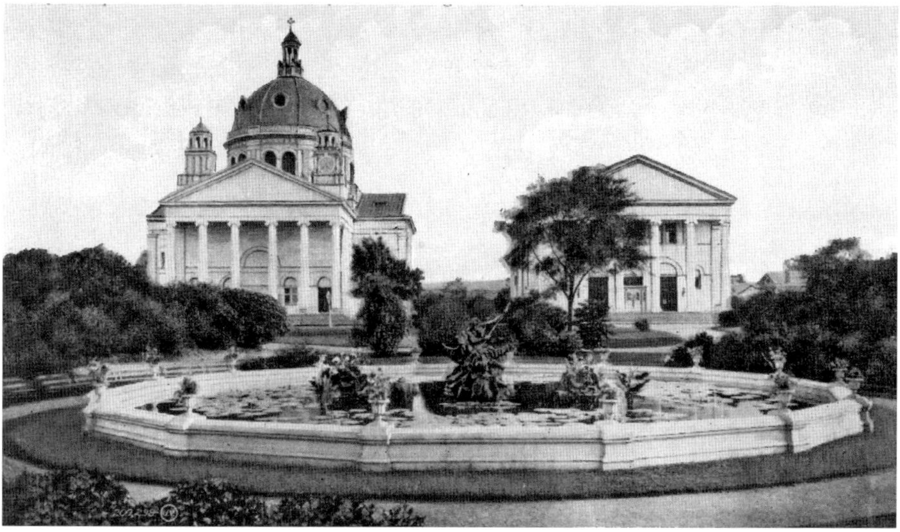

The church, music hall and fountain as they appear on the Sailors' Snug Harbor grounds. *New York Public Library Digital Collection.*

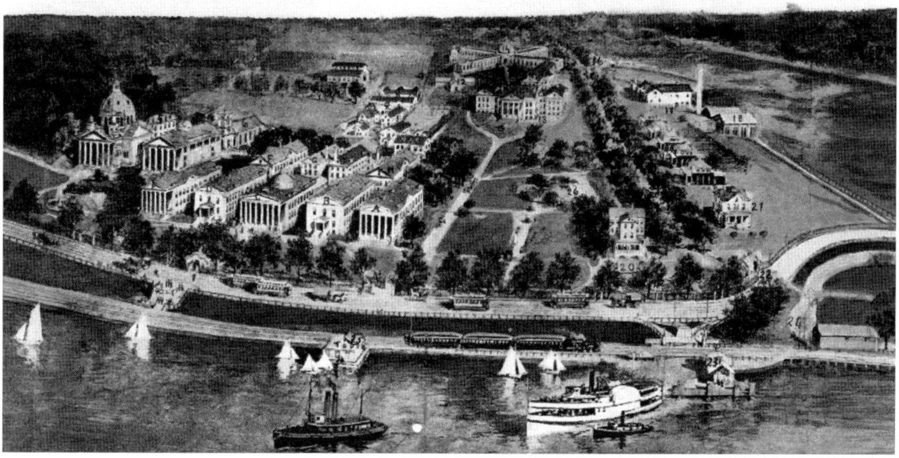

A bird's-eye view of Sailor's Snug Harbor. *New York Public Library Digital Collection.*

housing two hundred mariners, Snug Harbor's needs seemed to grow alongside the number of its buildings and inhabitants. At its peak, in 1880, over fifty-five buildings were located on the property, and Snug Harbor was home to one thousand retired merchants of the sea, as documented by Kate Feighery in "Robert Richard Randall and Sailor's Snug Harbor" at greenwichvillagehistory.wordpress.com.

The Snug Harbor Cemetery, located on the massive grounds once referred to as "Monkey Hill" by its residents, has over seven thousand sailors buried in it. Today, the majority of those who were laid to rest there are in unmarked graves because their headstones were removed during the 1980s and placed in storage for preservation. The cemetery is also home to some of Staten Island's most legendary ghost stories. Across from the cemetery lies a quaint lake that served as the water supply for the facility. Today, the cemetery is owned by Snug Harbor, but the lake and the land surrounding it is owned by the City of New York. The area is known as Alison Park and is abundant with wildlife and hiking trails.

On the grounds were also a 150-acre farm that produced all the food for the facility, a barn that housed its livestock and a six-hundred-seat music hall auditorium where entertainment was provided to the weary sailors. Sailors' Snug Harbor was truly an environment that enabled sailors to live the latter days of their lives comfortably and enjoyably.

A SAILOR'S LIFE

The requirements for residency at Sailors' Snug Harbor were to have spent five years at sea representing the United States or ten years at sea under a foreign flag; furthermore, there weren't any discriminations against religion, race or age. According to the Noble Maritime Collection at Snug Harbor Cultural Center, regardless of a mariner's rank at sea, all residents at the retirement home were referred to as "Captain" by its staff, and the retired seamen were treated with the utmost respect and dignity.

The residents of Sailors' Snug Harbor lived in dormitory-style rooms. The dormitory building, known as Building D, was designed with windows that allowed natural light to brightly filter into the living quarters. Two men resided in each room, were assigned their own bed and shared a dresser for their clothing. Upon entering the facility, they were examined by one of the Snug Harbor physicians and, pending their good health, were given a room in one of the eight dormitories on the property. Each sailor was provided

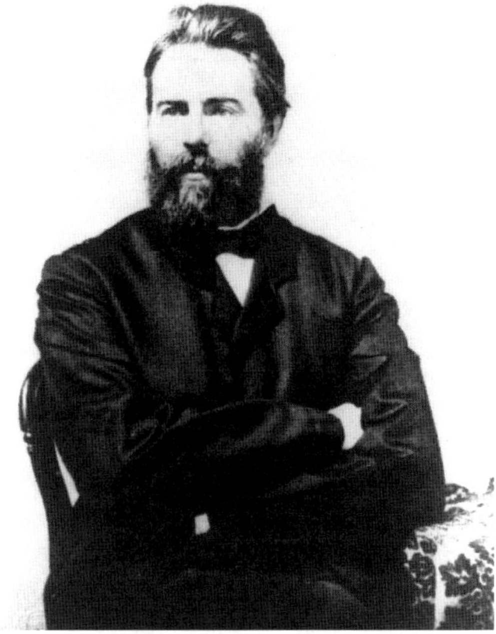

Left: Portrait of American author Herman Melville, brother of Captain Thomas Melville, former governor of Sailors' Snug Harbor. *Wikimedia Commons.*

Below: An illustration depicting good times for the sailors at Sailors' Snug Harbor's Music Hall. *Wikimedia Commons.*

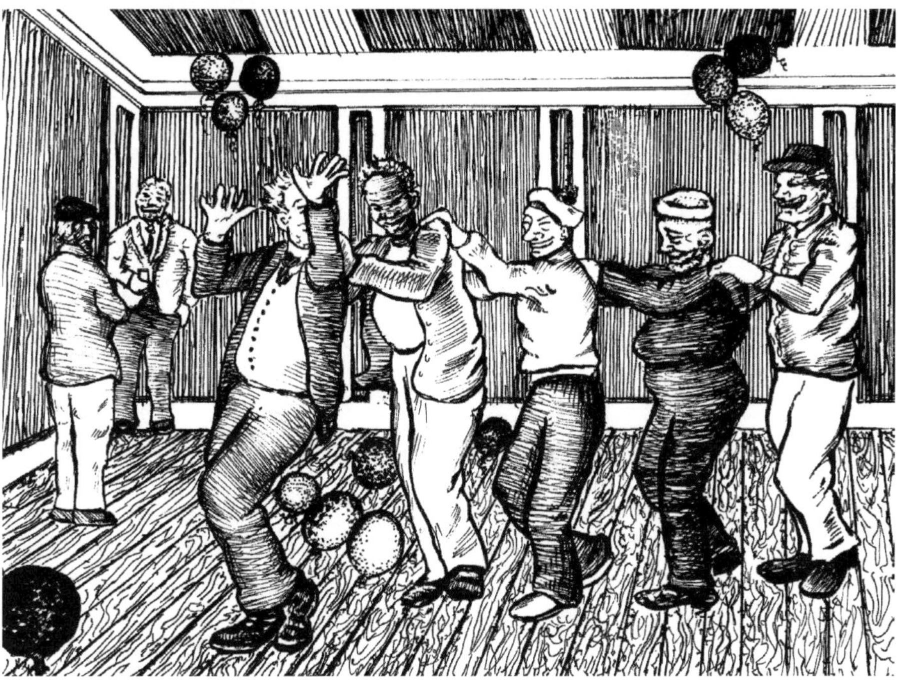

clothes for the winter and summer seasons (all monogrammed with the Snug Harbor logo, SSH), and although alcohol beverages were forbidden, lively entertainment was provided for them at the music hall. Able to come and go both on and off the premises as they desired, many sailors sold homemade handicrafts to obtain spending money, spent time fishing in the lakes and swam and boated off the nearby pier.

One of Snug Harbor's governors from 1867 to 1884 was Captain Thomas Melville, brother of American novelist Herman Melville. It is said that upon visiting his brother at Sailors' Snug Harbor and listening to the seafaring tales of the sea from the old men, Herman Melville found his inspiration to write his highly acclaimed book *Moby-Dick*.

THE BEGINNING OF THE END

By the late twentieth century, Sailors' Snug Harbor began to have some financial difficulties due to the dwindling number of sailors living on the property, as well as the vast improvement in social security and health benefits for the elderly in the United States, according to the article "Snug Harbor: A Port in the Storm" in *Bowery Boys: New York City History*. Sailors' Snug Harbor enrollment numbers fell drastically to a mere 110 by the 1970s versus the 1,000 in 1900. As a result of this decline, the need for a privately endowed retirement complex for mariners was coming to a close. A depleting clientele and loss of capital were signs of trouble ahead for the cherished retirement home.

The Snug Harbor trustees began to demolish many of the buildings, vehemently clearing the land with intentions to sell off the property to real estate developers. Preservationists, advocates and community leaders fought resiliently to save the historic buildings and preserve their century-old history. The hope was to garner landmark designation and build a cultural arts center with botanical gardens for the community to enjoy. After many legal battles, six of Sailors' Snug Harbor's buildings were listed in the National Register of Historic Places and designated landmarks; the plaques' seals read: "we who are weary seek a harbor," memorializing Captain Robert Richard Randall's mission. Also, as a tribute to his generosity, the neighborhood adjacent to Snug Harbor is known as Randall Manor today.

The 1976 *New York Times* article "Jacqueline Onassis Goes to Snug Harbor," by Edith Evans Asbury, mentions that Onassis, the director of the Municipal Art Society, was instrumental in obtaining the landmark goal and

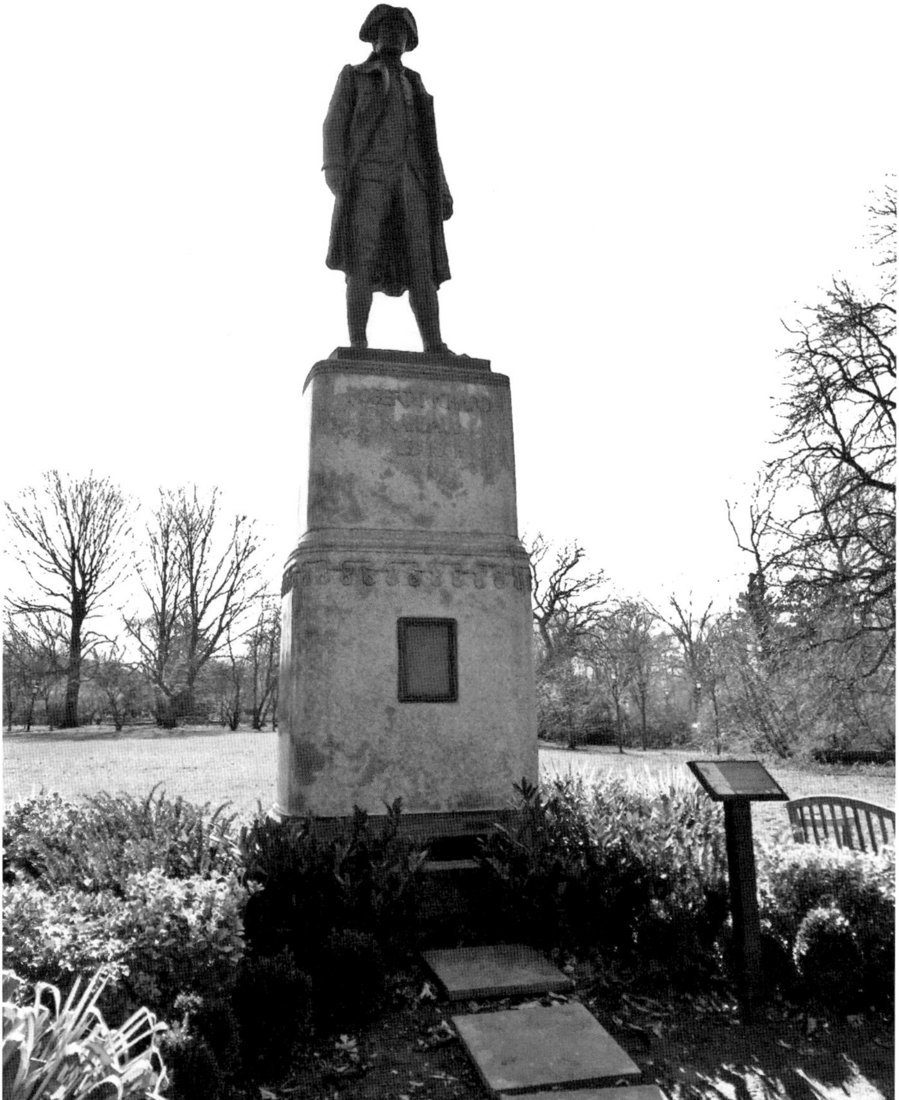

Modern-day photograph of the Robert Richard Randall Statue on the Snug Harbor Cultural Center and Botanical Garden grounds. *Author's collection.*

was an avid supporter of preserving the grounds. She visited the property, absorbed all its beauty and was quoted as saying to civic leaders and sponsors of the proposed cultural center who greeted her: "I have always been interested in the preservation of old buildings, even as a child....The more attention that can be attracted to this lovely place the better."

Michael Fressola's *Staten Island Advance* article "'Landmarks' on Staten Island: 11th Hour Triumph of History or Destruction by Development?" quotes Onassis as saying, "It's a sanctuary and it must be preserved." He further goes on to comment that Mayor John V. Lindsay was an advocate very much interested in the site becoming parkland as well. The City of New York purchased the land in 1976, and in September of the same year, Snug Harbor Cultural Center opened its gates to the public.

Resulting from the change of hands of the property, transitions occurred. The Snug Harbor trustees relocated the remaining sailors living at Sailors' Snug Harbor to a new site established in Sea Level, North Carolina. They also relocated the Saint-Gaudens statue of Randall there; however, a replica of the statue remains on the Snug Harbor grounds today in his honor.

Today, Sailors' Snug Harbor maintains offices in Manhattan, but the Snug Harbor trustees no longer operate a mariners' retirement home. They do, however, continue Robert Randall's mission in assisting mariners all over the country.

In 2008, the former site of Sailors' Snug Harbor became known to the community as Snug Harbor Cultural Center and Botanical Garden, a nonprofit organization and proud Smithsonian affiliate. Acting as an umbrella to its museums and gardens, it operates and manages the cultural center, its educational centers and its park.

A NEW START

Since 1976, Snug Harbor Cultural Center and Botanical Garden has evolved into a vibrant and thriving cultural center. Remaining true to the visions of its founding directors, the Cultural Center remains committed to preserving Snug Harbor's important history and restoring the historic grounds, as well as providing the community with myriad educational and recreational opportunities. With its distinctive museums, interactive exhibitions, artistic performances and intricately designed gardens, there is no doubt it is a wonderland for adults and children.

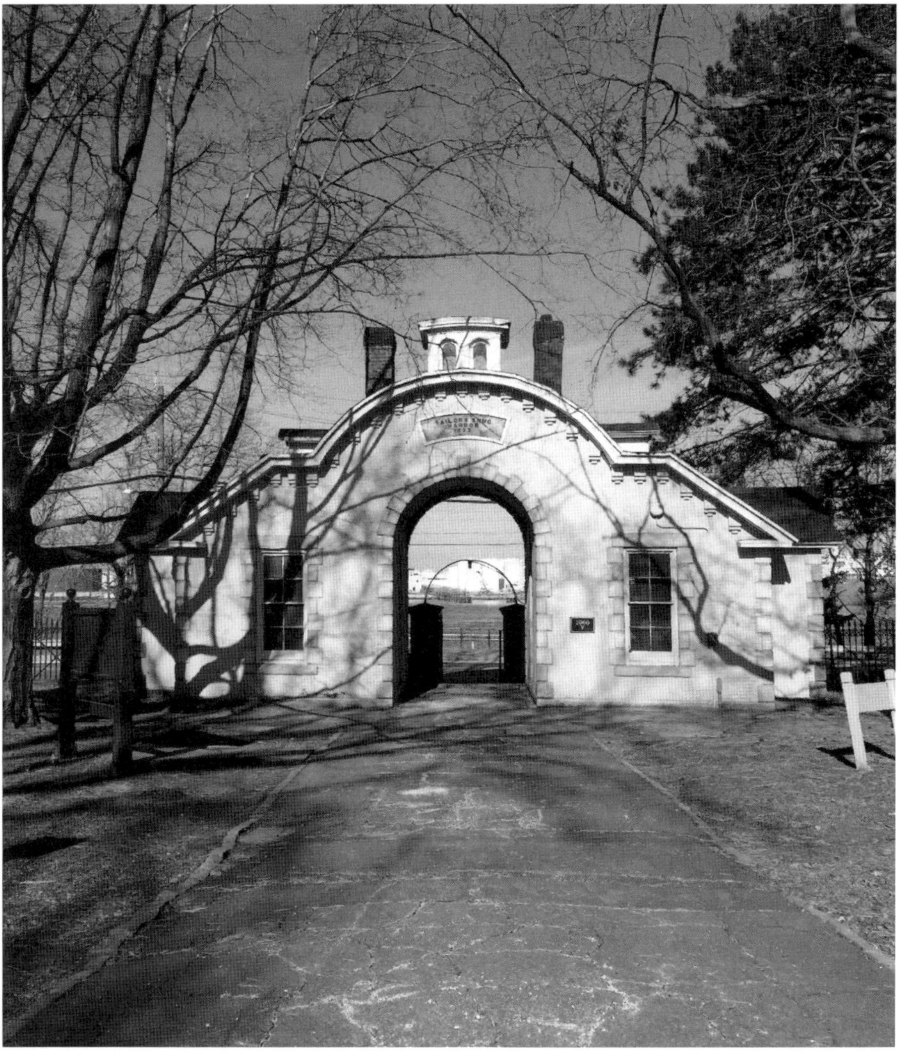

Modern-day photograph of the entrance to Snug Harbor Cultural Center and Botanical Garden. *Author's collection.*

In an enclave of oak trees and blossoming cherry trees, Snug Harbor is a hub of diversified activities for all to enjoy. It is hard to imagine that such an elaborate cultural center set in a peaceful environment exists so close to the noise and busy streets of Lower Manhattan. A true mecca to behold, it remains one of Staten Island's oldest and greatest treasures.

MUSEUMS AND THE PERFORMING ARTS

The museums at Snug Harbor are plentiful, indeed. The Cultural Center offers a bevy of museums to peruse, each unique in its own definitive way. Each museum hosts ongoing events, educational workshops, interactive and historical exhibits and diversified visual performances.

Newhouse Center for Contemporary Art

Established in 1977, the Newhouse Center for Contemporary Art has galleries devoted to art exhibits by both local and international artists. It also offers the opportunity for its artist-in-residence to exhibit his or her work.

The Newhouse Center for Contemporary Art and Snug Harbor's Visitor Center are located in the centerpiece building, known as Building C. It is one of the original five masterfully built Greek Revival structures. It is here where, at one time, the Sailors' Snug Harbor housed its administrative offices

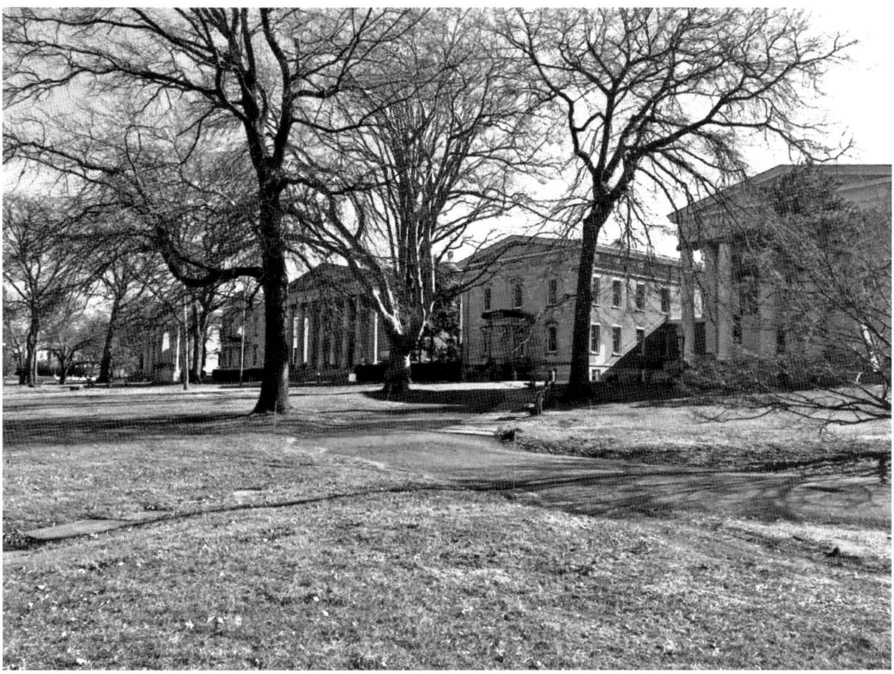

Modern-day photograph of the majestic "Front Five" buildings on the Snug Harbor Cultural Center and Botanical Garden grounds. *Author's collection.*

on the main floor, and its second floor was a dormitory for thirty-seven sailors. Building C remains as magnificent today as it was back then, and its neoclassical and Greek motif design are spectacular. Stained-glass transoms featuring ships and lighthouses adorn the spacious area, with a large transom above the entranceway honoring Robert Randall, founder of Sailors' Snug Harbor. The windows on the opposite ends of the room depict the sun and the moon, and the blue glass etchings in the upper clerestory are images of various constellations as a nod to a sailor's navigation of the seas. Delicately balanced throughout the ceiling mural are beautiful images of Neptune, ropes, anchors and even parrots. A large dome in the center of the ceiling allows for natural light to filter in, and a nautical compass is inlaid within the hardwood flooring, paying homage to the sailors who once called this home.

Noble Maritime Collection

Since the year 2000, the Noble Maritime Collection has found its home in one of the former splendid "Front Five" buildings, specifically Building D. After the extensive restoration of the debilitated twenty-eight-thousand-square-foot former sailors' dormitory, according to www.noblemaritime.org, a representative of the National Trust for Historic Preservation cites its preservation as "a particularly moving demonstration of citizen volunteers taking on a daunting preservation project and completing it with great style" and further quotes, "The Noble may be one of the nation's best examples of a volunteer restoration project."

The restoration project is the proud recipient of the 1999 New York Preservation Award from the Municipal Art Society of New York, the Preservation League Award and the President's Award from the Staten Island Chamber of Commerce. Within its beautiful setting, the Noble Maritime Collection takes great pride in offering exhibits that reflect the people who dedicated themselves to the working waterfront of New York Harbor and is a delight to those who love history.

It is named in honor of maritime artist John C. Noble (1913–1983), the son of the distinguished artist John "Wichita Bill" Noble. As a young man, John Noble spent many years observing his father's love of painting and drawing. Influenced by his father's talent and inheriting it, he went on to render and paint many of the ships, vessels and schooners in the New York Harbor and its surrounding waterways. From 1928 to 1945, he worked as a seaman on boats and in marine salvage, and it is there in the boat docks and their graveyard that he found his inspiration and the subjects of his artwork. He set off into the harbor in his houseboat made of salvaged pieces and artistically captured New York Harbor's twentieth-century marine industry. His gallery encompasses many pieces of his artwork, his writings and historical marine artifacts. A cornerstone in this collection is a replica of Noble's houseboat that depicts his art studio.

Another notable gallery within the museum is the Sailors' Snug Harbor exhibit. The incredible history of Sailors' Snug Harbor, extensive photographs and marine artifacts, including the replica of a dormitory room, complete with furniture dating back to the mid-1800s, provide insight into how sailors spent their final days at Snug Harbor.

In 2010, the Noble Maritime Collection took over the stewardship of the 1883 Robbins Reef Light Station, an off-shore brick-and-cast-iron lighthouse located between Staten Island's North Shore and the Statue of Liberty. This exhibition showcases the history of the lighthouse and the compelling story of its keeper, Katherine Walker (1848–1931), who maintained the duties as keeper of the lighthouse after her husband's death in 1890. Over the course of two decades, she tended to her family while still illuminating the lighthouse with kerosene lights in all types of weather. She dedicated her life to protecting the lives of sailors as they entered and exited New York Harbor.

In a 2007 *New York Sun* article entitled "A Home for Ancient Mariners," the museum is described as "an unsung gem among New York museums."

Today, the museum continues to cultivate exhibits and restoration projects that were pivotal in maritime history. Also on site are a printmaking studio and performance spaces.

Staten Island Museum

The Staten Island Museum may be relatively new to the Snug Harbor grounds, but its history dates back to over one hundred years ago, and since then, its mission hasn't wavered. As early as 1908, a group of naturalists from Staten Island documented the rapidly changing environment and became advocates in environmental preservation. Since 1908, the museum staff have worked together with the Audubon Society in annual bird counts and focus on the preservation and protection of the Island's parks. In 1918, the Institute of Arts and Sciences was incorporated, dedicated to archiving local history.

Since 2015, the Staten Island Museum has been located at the Snug Harbor Cultural Center. The museum is in Building A, one of the landmark

Greek Revival buildings. The highly anticipated renovation of the building's eighteen thousand square feet took four years to complete.

The museum is also the first historic landmark building on Staten Island to earn certification from the U.S. Green Building Council in Leadership in Energy and Environmental Design (LEED). The building maintains its historical stairwells, windows, roof and exterior walls, while its interior meets the environmental standards set by the American Museum Association. The museum offers the public a classroom space for educational purposes and an auditorium, and its galleries represent dynamic exhibits focusing on biodiversity, natural history and world art.

Additionally, Building H is home to the Staten Island Museum History Center & Archives. It is here that historians work tirelessly, dedicating their efforts to the preservation of Staten Island's detailed history. Everything from hundred-year-old maps and nineteenth-century photographs to the written journals of some of the Island's most distinguished inhabitants are archived for future generations.

Staten Island Children's Museum

The Staten Island Children's Museum is an exciting museum where creativity and curiosity are nurtured and encouraged. Offering a collection of hands-on exhibits, such as a bug and insect collection, a theatrical playhouse and an indoor pirate ship, there is no doubt this museum is a favorite of Snug Harbor's youngest visitors.

The museum sits adjacent to a great lawn and pavilion used for outdoor play and educational performances. Its main building dates back to 1913 and is connected via a modern walkway to what once was the barn from Sailors' Snug Harbor.

Visual Arts

The Green Gallery and the Commons Gallery also reside on the Cultural Center's property. They offer performance space and studios for emerging artists and curators. The galleries are home to diversified exhibits, artistic workshops, educational lectures and SHARP (the Snug Harbor Artist Residency Program).

Performing Arts

Snug Harbor Cultural Center and Botanical Garden is dedicated to bringing the best of film, dance, stage and song to the community. With events throughout the year, its performing arts programs are held in the historic music hall.

THE BOTANICAL GARDEN

The Snug Harbor Cultural Center is home to Staten Island Botanical Garden, where a collection of nine elaborately themed gardens are maintained. The gardens and their designs are inspired from all over the world, and their stunning displays of foliage and flowers grace the grounds with beauty and fragrance. Each garden, elegantly and intricately designed, is adorned by fountains, trellises, reflecting pools and sculptures. Horticulture walks are offered seasonally, providing visitors with information about each garden's botanical symbolism and arrangements. Whether seeking a quiet, serene setting to relax and breathe in the fresh air or quenching a gardener's thirst in learning about the variations of greenery and flowers, the Staten Island Botanical Garden is a must-see. Regardless of which garden you visit, it is certain you will be impressed by its floral display and style.

New York Chinese Scholar's Garden

The New York Chinese Scholar's Garden is magnificently designed as a compilation of the types of gardens in China. With structures built to resemble the mountains that inspired the paintings and poetry of Confucian, Buddhist and Taoist monks, and a fifteen-foot scholar's rock formation towering in the center of the courtyard, this garden is breathtaking, astounding and tranquil. It affords visitors the opportunity to explore multiple pavilions, a koi pond, stunning waterfalls and a bamboo forest path.

The White Garden

The White Garden is based on designs reminiscent of a European court garden, and this one is specifically influenced by Vita Sackville-West's

English garden Sissinghurst. The White Garden's design consists of plants containing pure white blossoms with gray and green foliage. These plants are intricately and carefully woven into garden lattices, growing into beautiful vibrant clusters of white and green.

Allée

Allée is the French word for "avenue," and this tunneled archway in the Botanical Garden is designed as such. It is predominantly green foliage accompanied by 120 hornbeams intertwined within an archway. Structures such as the Allée are commonly seen in European gardens. There, as well as here in the Botanical Garden, they cover walkways and paths, making the visitor's journey more enjoyable to the senses.

The Richmond County Savings Foundation Tuscan Garden

The Richmond County Savings Foundation Tuscan Garden is truly a unique garden. Its structure offers visitors an opportunity to enjoy an enclosed winter garden, as well as an outdoor amphitheater with grand lawns. The winter garden is decorated with a variety of topiaries, with potted olive and lemon trees nestled among water elements. Its design and inspiration come from a formal garden in Florence, Italy.

The Rose Garden

The Rose Garden is a gorgeous collection of more than one hundred varieties of enchantingly colorful roses. With its reflecting pool, the Rose Garden guarantees visitors a calming and peaceful environment. A bronze sculpture of a heron drying its wings adorns the pool as well. The Rose Garden commemorates rosarian gardener Clare Lambert.

The Connie Gretz Secret Garden

The Connie Gretz Secret Garden is inspired by Frances Hodgson Burnett's classic story *The Secret Garden*. A labyrinth in design, this garden is a delightful maze of intricate paths and most fun to its young visitors. Hedges of greenery, trails of flowers and walls of boxwoods create a magnificent puzzle that encompass more than half an acre. Its design is based on European influences.

Carl Grillo Glass House

The Carl Grillo Glass House garden is actually built on the site of the original Sailors' Snug Harbor greenhouse. Having been expanded over the years, today this large, enclosed greenhouse is used for the exhibition and propagation of rare and stunning plants. The structure has a unique heating system that is able to create arid, tropical and temperate climates, enabling the plants to grow and flowers to thrive.

The Perennial Garden

The Perennial Garden is adjacent to the Carl Grillo Glass House. Designed in 2000, the garden continues to grow and thrive each year. The perennial plants come in an assortment of vibrant colors and shades of foliage. They are mostly used as borders outlining walkways or as accent plants within a garden. Being seasonal plants, different perennials thrive during the seasons. Today, the Perennial Garden at the Botanical Garden is a year-round garden to appreciate and enjoy.

The Healing Garden

The Healing Garden is a living memorial to the Staten Islanders who perished on September 11, 2001. This serene garden sits on a hillside overlooking twenty acres in the distance. Under the canopy of one hundred trees lies a combination of hardwoods, green shrubbery and flowering perennials that grace this peaceful garden. The large quantity of trees symbolizes life and renewal.

Chapter 4

Notable Staten Islanders

Anna Leonowens

The English governess everyone knows from the iconic "Shall We Dance?" scene in *The King and I* was Anna Leonowens. The classic film and stage play were based on Margaret Landon's novel *Anna and the King of Siam* (1944), which was derived from Leonowens's memoirs, *The English Governess at the Siamese Court* and *The Romance of the Harem*, which she wrote while living on Staten Island after her five years in what is now Thailand working for King Mongkut in the 1860s.

In *Legends, Stories and Folklore of Old Staten Island* by Charles Gilbert Hine and William T. Davis, they include an essay by Mary Otis (Gay) Wilcox, who wrote:

> *A few years after the Civil War there arrived in our midst a stranger, an Englishwoman, and provided with most ample letters of introduction. These letters were to Mrs. William Templeton Johnson of Bement Avenue, but once met, no letters of introduction were necessary to establish Mrs. Leonowens among us as one of the most gracious and charming of personalities.*

She goes on to describe her as a brunette with wavy hair, "parted above a pair of brilliant, eager, searching eyes, rather a tanned skin and a warm-hearted, affectionate manner which endeared her to all who met her."

She completely charmed her new neighbors. "It was a red letter day when Mrs. Leonowens came to call and more especially when she was invited to a meal. Conversation was always lively, then, and most interesting, even if a bit over the head of the youngest member of the family, and there were sure to be references to, and stories of, Eastern life, full of interest and thrills of adventure equal to those found in the best of our books."

The author states that Leonowens had been widowed by a British army officer of Welsh heritage in India prior to the post in Siam and took it to help raise her two young children, a daughter named Avis and a son named Henry. She sent her daughter home to England to be educated during her tenure in Asia but took her son along for the adventure.

Leonowens is described by the writer as "brilliant with an aggressive personality," and she credits her with the reforms the Crown Prince of Siam Chulalongkorn undertook after his more traditional father's death.

"Why she chose Staten Island as a residence, I do not know; perhaps her thought was to be near New York." Leonowens set up residence in a home on the corner of Richmond Terrace and Tompkins Place in what was then called Factoryville and established a school for young children. This time, Avis accompanied her and helped her run the program as the main teacher. Her son was sent to England for school.

Many islanders enrolled as pupils, they say, some so small and who lived so far that they were pulled to the school on sleighs.

"Here Mrs. Leonowens wrote her books, and also from here she began to go about delivering lectures on Siam and the East. This, I fancy was her real business, for I remember absences on lecture tours throughout the neighboring States; and everywhere she made friends, people who grew to love and admire her until the day of her death."

Even after Leonowens left the Island for Nova Scotia, she honored the friendships she made here:

> *Some years after Mrs. Leonowens left the Island, one of the 81 children whose education she had undertaken in Siam arrived in New York on his way around the world, attended by a suitable suite of Siamese nobles and heralded by all the newspapers. Mrs. Leonowens came down from Halifax, where she then lived, to meet his Royal Highness. A large reception was given by the Prince and Mrs. Leonowens by Mrs. Vincenzo Botta, and Mrs. Leonowens sent invitations to her old Staten Island friends.*

Wilcox says it was her good fortune to be invited. She wore her finest silk dress to the party, with a little bonnet to match, and she was "scared nearly to death. I heard my name announced at Mrs. Botta's awesome drawing room door.

"Mrs. Leonowens took my hand and presented me to the Prince, rapidly speaking in Siamese and as rapidly translating that I had been an old pupil of hers. He bowed and placing a pointing finger on his chest, said in English, 'I, too! I, too!'"

Tragedy would strike when Leonowens's son died, leaving two small children he had with an Indian princess. The governess, ever resilient and able with children, raised them with the help of an Indian nurse.

Leonowens's books and the dramatizations are still banned in Thailand for depicting the king as backward. While she appreciated his culture and intelligence, she despised the slavery she saw there. The Thai, conversely, celebrate their king for keeping out English imperialism.

A book by Susan Morgan titled *Bombay Anna: The Real Story and Remarkable Adventures of the* King and I *Governess* tells a more nuanced story about Leonowens's social ambition and time in Siam.

Rodgers and Hammerstein immortalized the story in the 1951 play *The King and I*. It ran for three years at the St. James Theater, winning Tony Awards for Best Musical, Best Actress and Best Featured Actor, and has enjoyed many revivals.

Yul Brynner, who played the king in the original play, went on to star with Deborah Kerr in the musical film adaptation in 1956 by 20th Century Fox. The movie was nominated for nine Academy Awards and won five, including Best Actor for Brynner.

Leonowens died in Canada at the age of eighty-five.

ICHABOD CRANE

For lovers of ghost stories internationally, Ichabod Crane is the very superstitious schoolmaster who moves from Connecticut to New York State to educate the children of Sleepy Hollow, New York, near Tarry Town (now Tarrytown). He becomes terrified of the "Headless Horseman" (a Hessian soldier said to have been beheaded by a cannonball in an American Revolutionary War battle) in the woods on the way home from a failed attempt to become engaged one night.

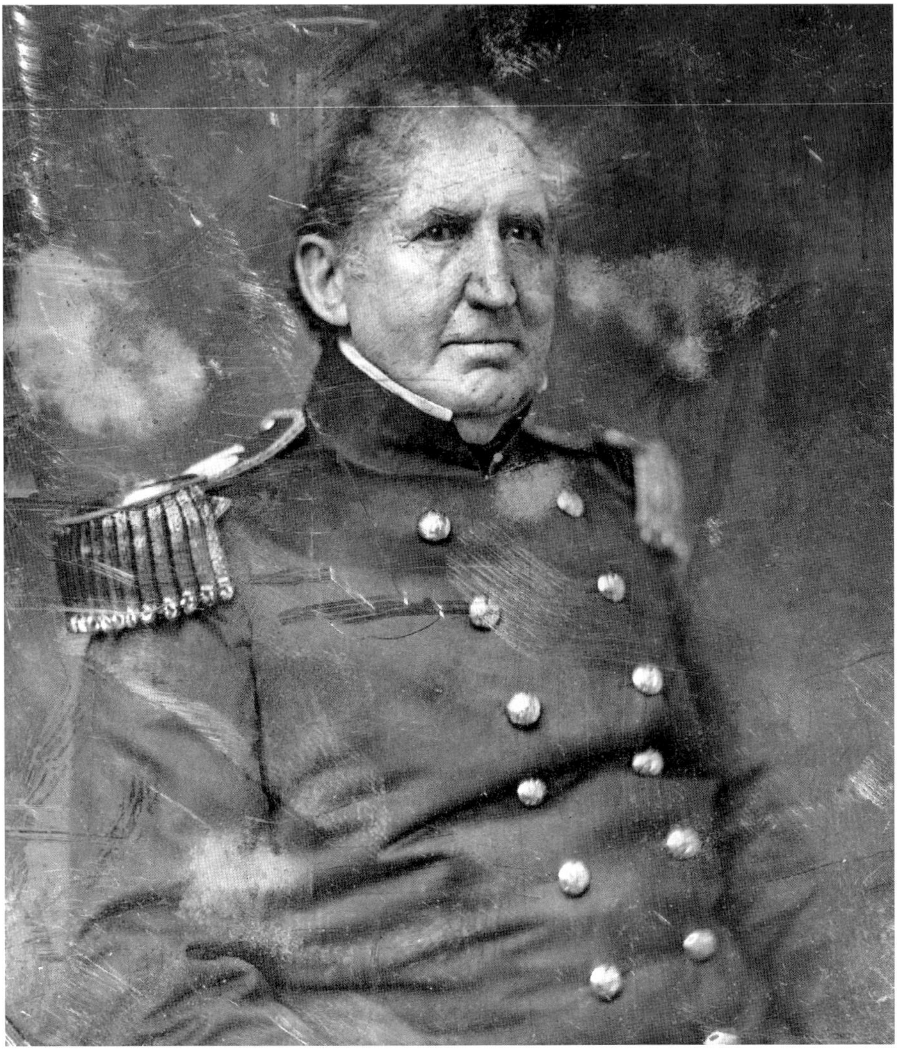

Ichabod Crane, who inspired author Washington Irving. *Wikimedia Commons.*

The timeless story by Washington Irving is "The Legend of Sleepy Hollow." Published in 1819 and 1820, it was part of a collection of essays and short stories called *The Sketch Book of Geoffrey Crayon, Gent*, commonly referred to as *The Sketch Book*. An excerpt follows:

> *On mounting a rising ground, which brought the figure of his fellow-traveler in relief against the sky, gigantic in height, and muffled in a cloak, Ichabod*

> *was horror-struck on perceiving that he was headless!—but his horror was still more increased on observing that the head, which should have rested on his shoulders, was carried before him on the pommel of his saddle!*

Crane has been portrayed by legendary actors, from Will Rogers to Jeff Goldblum to Ed Begley Jr. to Johnny Depp.

However, Ichabod Crane was a real person, born on July 18, 1787, in Elizabethtown (now Elizabeth), New Jersey. He was a graduate of West Point who served in the United States Army for forty-eight years, rising to the rank of colonel. He served two years in the United States Marine Corps prior to that. After the Mexican-American War, he and his wife, Charlotte, purchased a farm at Victory Boulevard and Signs Road, now in the New Springville section of the borough in 1850. He died only seven years later. His home was, sadly, demolished in the 1990s. He is buried at the nearby Asbury Cemetery in Bull's Head. His tombstone is a tall white obelisk that can be found in the back of the cemetery. The engraving there states that he served his country faithfully and was much beloved by all who knew him. Irving possibly "borrowed" the colonel's name after meeting him in 1814 in Sackets Harbor, New York, following the War of 1812, during which Colonel Crane served on the Niagara frontier.

As for the rest of the classic character beyond the name, Irving is said to have based him on Jesse Merwin, a teacher he had met who taught at the local schoolhouse in Kinderhook, New York, farther north up the Hudson River. Irving spent several months there in 1809. Alternately, he could be based on another educator, Samuel Youngs.

In a *New York Times* interview in 2015, Elizabeth I. Bradley, Irving scholar and editor of a new edition of *The Legend of Sleepy Hollow and Other Stories*, said she could find no proof of a meeting between Irving and Merwin in either *The Life and Letters of Washington Irving* (edited by Irving's nephew Pierre) or in two recent biographies of Irving. Dr. Bradley wrote:

> *I can say that Irving was fond of manufacturing "Yankee" names, which he had done since before the War of 1812 (when he may have met Ichabod Crane). In his 1809* A History of New York, *which, like "The Legend," is "narrated" by Irving's fictional Diedrich Knickerbocker, he describes New York being invaded by a "squatting, bundling, guessing, questioning, swapping, pumpkin-eating, molasses-daubing, shingle-splitting, cider-watering, horse-jockeying, notion-peddling crew" of Yankees with names like "Preserved Fish, and Habakkuk Nutter, and Return*

> *Strong, and Zerubbabel Fisk, and Determined Cock." (Preserved Fish was the name of a real New Yorker.)*

Dr. Bradley also told the *Times*:

> *Several 19th-century schoolteachers are held up as the model for the character of Ichabod Crane, including Samuel Youngs and Jesse Merwin. Kinderhook, the Columbia County town where Mr. Merwin taught, has renamed an extant 19th-century, one-room schoolhouse the Ichabod Crane Schoolhouse, the better to capitalize on the Irving legacy.*
>
> *It shows you how quick New Yorkers are to claim a piece of Irving's "Legend" for their own community. Much like George Washington, we all want to say that the Headless Horseman Slept Here.*

Along with its companion piece, "Rip Van Winkle," the story is considered a classic of American literature and Romanticism.

CHARLES GOODYEAR

Charles Goodyear, a hardware merchant originally from Philadelphia, had done a few stints in debtors' prison and had been lectured by his brother-in-law on taking better care of his children by the time he landed on Staten Island in 1836.

According to an article in *Reader's Digest* showcased on the Goodyear Corporate website about the inventor, the man who would become America's first rubber manufacturer was inspired to create a better product when trying to sell a valve he had created for rubber life preservers on a previous trip to New York in the summer of 1834:

> *The manager shook his head sadly. The company wasn't in the market for valves now; it would be lucky to stay in business at all.*
>
> *He showed Goodyear why: rack on rack of rubber goods which had been melted to malodorous glue by the torrid weather. In the company's factory at Roxbury, Mass., he confided, thousands of melted rubber articles were being returned by outraged customers. The directors had met in the dead of night to bury $20,000 worth of stinking rejects in a pit.*

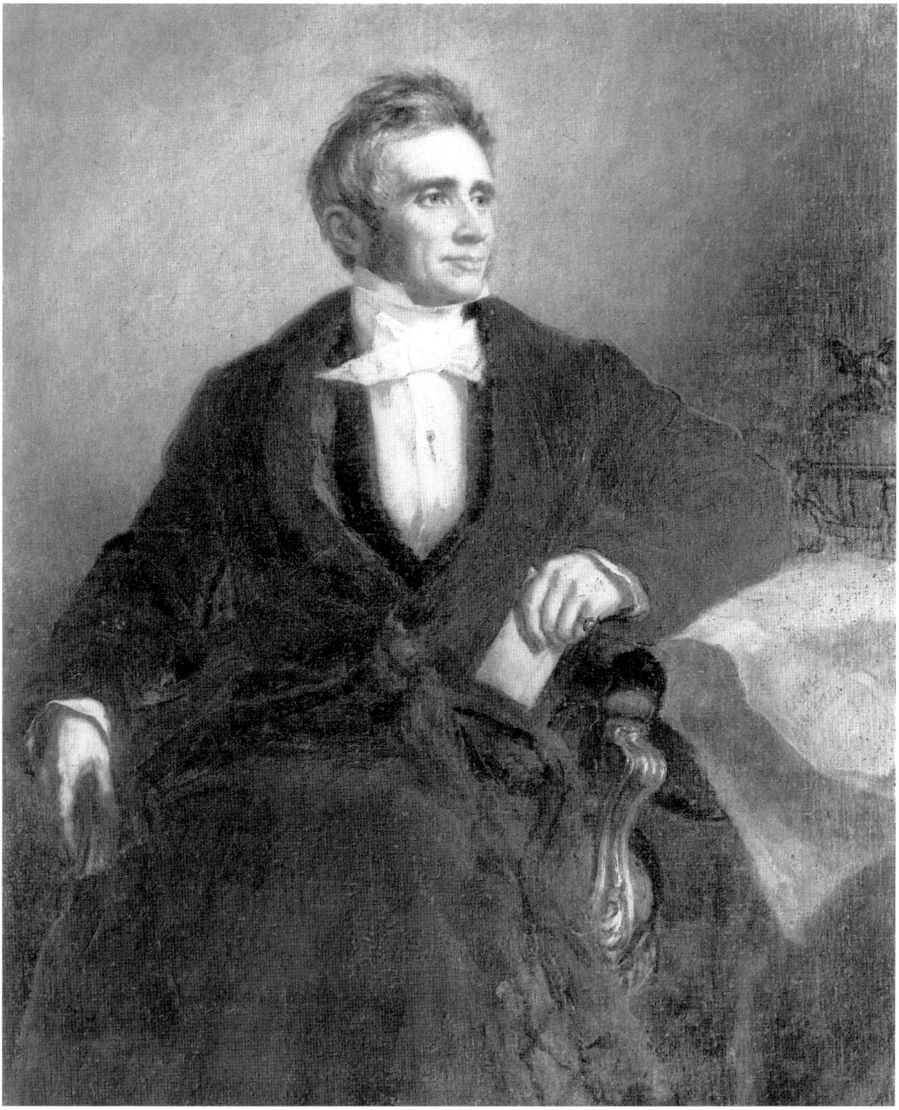

Rubber entrepreneur Charles Goodyear. *Library of Congress.*

While there had been a "rubber fever" in the early 1830s, it all ended when the product simply melted. The public rejected the product, and many factories shut down; investors lost fortunes. But Goodyear was inspired. "There is probably no other inert substance," he would say later, "which so excites the mind."

Undeterred by yet another stint in prison upon his return to Philadelphia, Goodyear asked his wife to bring him a batch of rubber and a rolling pin, and he worked in his cell on his first experiments with the raw material.

It occurred to him that some sort of dry powder could be added to the substance to keep it from becoming sticky when warm. When he got out of jail, he convinced a childhood friend to invest in more research. He added drying agents like magnesia and quicklime to the rubber and was even awarded a medal at a New York trade show for his efforts.

The eccentric inventor liked to paint, gild or emboss his products. When one day he wanted to reuse an old sample he'd painted bronze, he used nitric acid. The piece turned black, and he discarded it. But a couple of days later, he picked it out of his trash and realized it was smooth and dry—he'd solved the problem! While he now drew investment, a financial panic wiped out his backer and the budding business. Goodyear and his family lived during this time in his abandoned rubber factory on Staten Island and ate fish they caught in the harbor.

He attracted investment again, and his fortune went up and down a few more times—he discovered sulfur was even better for fixing rubber—before he neglected to file for proper patents on time.

He died in 1860, $200,000 in debt. Later, his family did profit from accumulated royalties.

Neither Goodyear nor his family was ever connected with the company named in his honor, today's billion-dollar Goodyear Tire & Rubber Co., the world's largest rubber business. Goodyear's only direct descendant among modern companies is United States Rubber, which years ago absorbed a small company he once served as director.

"Today there is a cultivated rubber tree for every two human beings on earth," says *Reader's Digest*. "Three million tree 'milkers' harvest the crop. The United States alone imports almost half of it, and synthesizes as much or more from petroleum. The whole huge apparatus owes its existence to the invincible little fanatic who might have died a bitter man, but didn't.

"'Life,' he wrote, 'should not be estimated exclusively by the standard of dollars and cents. I am not disposed to complain that I have planted and others have gathered the fruits. A man has cause for regret only when he sows and no one reaps.'"

Mary Outerbridge

"Think tennis in New York and Queens comes to mind, either the National Tennis Center in Flushing Meadows–Corona Park…or the West Side Tennis Club in Forest Hills," wrote the *New York Times* in an article in 2010. "Tennis as we know it, though, started on Staten Island, where what was billed as the first game was played in 1874 and where the first national grand tournament was held."

That first game of tennis in the United States was played between Mary Ewing Outerbridge and her sister Laura of New Brighton on an hourglass-shaped court.

According to Bermuda.com, when Mary returned to her Staten Island home from a holiday in her parents' ancestral Bermuda in 1874,

> *she had trouble getting through customs in New York. In her luggage the customs inspectors had found some curious objects—a long, narrow net, which did not look like a fishing net, and several implements with handles and webbed heads. Could they be rug beaters, butterfly catchers or perhaps snowshoes?*
>
> *Miss Outerbridge explained that this was the equipment needed for a new outdoor game called Sphairistiké. A few weeks later this new game—clearly neither cricket nor baseball—was played at the Staten Island Cricket and Baseball Club. Across a net hung between two posts, gentlemen and ladies could be seen hitting a bouncing rubber ball with some sort of bat. Sphairistiké (as it was first known) had come to America.*

The International Tennis Hall of Fame states that "while are there several claimants for the introduction of tennis in the United States, and the identity remains open to debate, there is no doubt that Mary Ewing Outerbridge played a significant role in the game that made its American debut in 1874."

The New Brighton, Staten Island resident originally from Philadelphia is called the "Mother of American Tennis" by many historians. The hall of fame writes:

> *Reports of her actions suggest that while she was vacationing in Bermuda during the winter of 1874 she noticed some British army officers in a distant corner of a cricket field playing lawn tennis. Walter Clopton Wingfield's boxed lawn tennis set (called Sphairistiké—Greek for "playing ball") had been patented in England on February 23, 1874 and a few months later several sets were sent to Bermuda for use by men stationed*

> *there. The Outerbridge family relates that Mary played the game while in Bermuda and when she returned to Staten Island, New York in the spring of 1874, she brought back some of the equipment that had been given to her by the British officers.*

She also drew a diagram of a proper court.

Shortly thereafter, she set up a game at the Staten Island Cricket and Baseball Club. "Some mystery remains, however, as the earliest account on record of Outerbridge's introduction of the game is from 1887," according to the international organization in honor of the sport. Nevertheless, they inducted her into their hall of fame in 1981.

Mary Ewing Outerbridge was only thirty-four when she died of Bright's disease—a condition causing chronic inflammation of the kidneys—in 1886. She is buried in Silver Mount Cemetery on Staten Island, next to her parents.

The Outerbridge family has another claim to fame: Staten Island's southernmost bridge to New Jersey spanning the Arthur Kill is named for Mary's brother, Eugenius, a Staten Island industrialist and the first chairman of the Port of New York Authority. He was also instrumental in organizing the first tennis tournaments on Staten Island.

DONALD TRUMP

Donald John Trump, the forty-fifth president of the United States, was born in Jamaica, Queens, and spent many formative years on Staten Island as a journeyman to his Realtor father, Fred.

It may be said that he did his own real estate apprenticeship here, much like the reality TV show he hosted, shadowing his father around properties they owned in New Dorp and on Grymes Hill and performing jobs such as painting, cleaning the Venetian blinds and emptying the coin boxes in the laundry rooms.

The landlords were so well liked here that a fan club called the "Trumpeteers" developed among senior women in the Grymes Hill properties. Fred Trump had put aside a free apartment there for the women, who were mostly widows, to meet. He also sent buses for them to take them on trips to Atlantic City.

Trump liked to dine at the casual Ann's Sugar Bowl and get in a round of golf at Silver Lake Golf Course in those days. He traveled to Staten

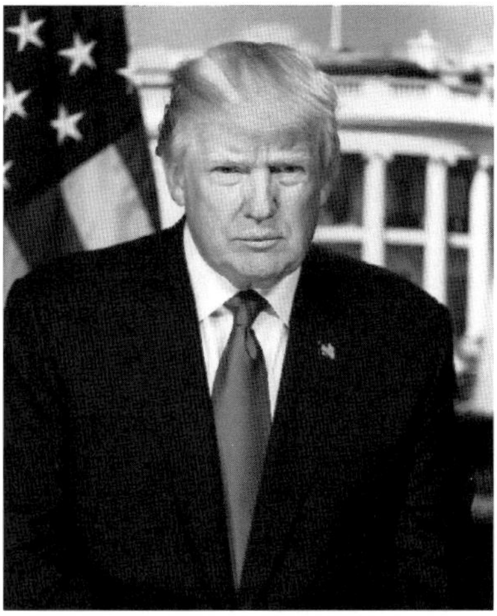

President Donald J. Trump. *Official White House portrait, public domain.*

Island on the former ferry from Brooklyn and recalled thinking the waves were so high as he crossed the Narrows to Staten Island.

Trump visited Staten Island many more times, speaking at PS 69 in New Springville, visiting the Trumpeteer social club, giving the commencement address at Wagner College and campaigning for president.

Time magazine reported on one such campaign stop at the Hilton Garden Inn, where Trump was hailed as a hometown hero. "When Maria Andrews' mother came home with a load of heavy groceries and found a broken elevator at the modest brick Tysens Park Apartments on Staten Island, she wasn't expecting to get much help from building management," they wrote. "But then she saw Fred Trump pull up in an elegant black limousine. She put down her groceries and rapped on the limo's tinted window to complain to the real estate royal who owned her building. To her surprise, the elder Trump came out and helped her carry her groceries up five flights of stairs, Andrews says today—and he stayed for coffee."

Andrews remembered seeing Fred and Donald strolling around her childhood apartment complex, chatting with her mother. "He was just a nice man," Andrews told *Time* of Fred Trump. "And Donald was with him a lot. So I was a fan of them from back then."

Trump was quoted that day as saying he would spend summers on Staten Island with his father and how Staten Islanders were "the greatest people."

"We love Staten Island. We love New York," Trump said at the Staten Island press conference at his rally, accompanied by members of the New York Veteran Police Association, which had recently endorsed him for the GOP nomination. "This is just an amazing place." He cited the relative safety of Staten Island, adding, "We have great police, great people on Staten Island and I know it so well."

While Staten Island has more registered Democrats than Republicans, the latter usually win the vote due to higher voter turnout. That was the case in the 2016 presidential race, when Trump received 57 percent of the vote here compared to 40 percent for Hillary Clinton.

Dorothy Day

Though she once said, "Don't call me a saint. I don't want to be dismissed so easily," Dorothy Day, a founder of the *Catholic Worker* newspaper and social justice movement who lived a simple life in a bungalow in the former Spanish Camp in the Annadale section of Staten Island, is under consideration for posthumous canonization.

James Parker wrote in the March 2017 issue of *Atlantic Monthly*:

> *Whether or not the Catholic Church makes it official—and the cause for her canonization rumbles on—Dorothy Day was most definitely a saint.* Is *a saint, because her holiness has suffered no decrease in vitality since her death, at age 83, in 1980, and her example, her American example, is more challenging and provocative today than it ever was. Day was about people, especially poor people, especially those whom she called with some wryness "the undeserving poor," and the paramount importance of serving them. For her, what the Church defines as Works of Mercy—feeding the hungry, visiting the sick, sheltering the homeless, and so on—were not pious injunctions or formulas for altruism but physical principles, as inevitable as the first law of thermodynamics. Pare her right down to her pith, strip away all her history and biography, and what do you get? A fierce set of cheekbones and a command to love. That's the legacy of Dorothy Day, and it is endless.*

Born in Brooklyn Heights on November 8, 1897, Dorothy Day was an activist who worked for such social causes as pacifism and women's suffrage through the prism of the Catholic Church, according to Biography.com.

After a young, bohemian adulthood spent in Greenwich Village writing for several small newspapers, she converted in 1927 and was baptized on Staten Island in order to raise her daughter, Tamar Teresa, in the church. She co-founded the *Catholic Worker* newspaper in 1933, and its advocacy journalism in favor of Catholic values, such as caring for the poor, was so successful that it led to a successful movement by the same name.

She was a radical activist, arrested several times for her protests for pacifism and women's suffrage. The author of several books was extremely articulate, with phrases that live to this day, such as, "The greatest challenge of the day is: how to bring about a revolution of the heart, a revolution which has to start with each one of us."

"Dorothy Day dedicated much of her life in service to her socialist beliefs and her adopted faith. She died on November 29, 1980, in New York City, at Maryhouse—one of the Catholic settlement houses she had helped establish. The movement she created continues to thrive to this day, with more than 200 communities across the United States and another 28 communities abroad," according to Biography.com.

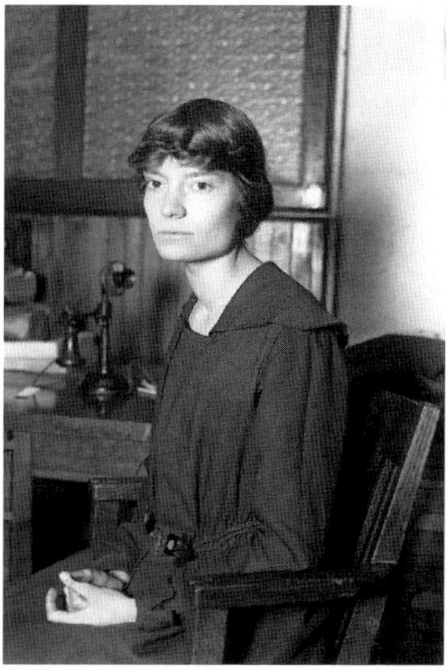

Founder of the Catholic Workers movement, Dorothy Day. *Wikimedia Commons.*

She is buried in Resurrection Cemetery in Pleasant Plains, not far from where she lived. Her bungalow has since been destroyed to make way for luxury homes.

In 2015, Pope Francis referred to her as one of "four great Americans," alongside Abraham Lincoln, Martin Luther King Jr. and Thomas Merton.

Her granddaughter Kate Hennessy published a book titled *Dorothy Day: The World Will Be Saved by Beauty: An Intimate Portrait of My Grandmother* in early 2017.

AMY VANDERBILT

"We must learn which ceremonies may be breached occasionally at our convenience and which ones may never be if we are to live pleasantly with our fellow man," said etiquette expert Amy Vanderbilt, born on Staten Island on July 22, 1908.

The legendary inspiration toward more polite living published *Amy Vanderbilt's Complete Book of Etiquette* in 1952, a book that, according to Britanica.com, has been called a "guide to gracious living." It sold millions of copies and is still in circulation as *Amy Vanderbilt's Etiquette.*

In her classic introduction, she wrote:

> *Who needs a book of etiquette? Everyone does. The simplest family, if it hopes to move just a little into a wider world, needs to know at least the elementary rules. Even the most sophisticated man or woman used to a great variety of social demands cannot hope to remember every single aspect of*

> *etiquette applying to even one possible social contingency. The human mind is so constructed that even if a person were to read through a book such as this from cover to cover he could retain only that information that had interest for him at the time of reading. Consciously, at least, the rest would be discarded as irrelevant to his way of life. But let some new way of living open up for him a move from city to country, a trip to a new part of the world and his etiquette book becomes his reference book, ready to piece out his own store of information.*

Often referred to as "the successor to Emily Post" (who also lived on Staten Island), Vanderbilt hosted the television program *It's in Good Taste*, which aired from 1954 to 1960, and also had a radio show titled *The Right Thing to Do* from 1960 to 1962. She also had a popular syndicated newspaper advice column.

Among the organizations where she worked as a consultant on protocol was the U.S. Department of State. In addition to her book on etiquette, Vanderbilt also authored volumes on cooking.

Despite a charmed life, Vanderbilt had a tragic death. She "fell or jumped to her death last night from a second-story window of her residence at 438 East 87th Street," according to police quoted in her 1974 *New York Times* obituary. Friends and relatives said she had frequent dizzy spells due to hypertension medicine, and it remains a mystery whether she fell or committed suicide.

She was only sixty-six years old and was pronounced dead on arrival at Metropolitan Hospital after her body was found lying near the front steps of the four-story building by a man walking by. Her husband and youngest son were home at the time of the tragedy.

Vanderbilt was a first cousin of Commodore Cornelius Vanderbilt, the railroad magnate, and descended from America's first Vanderbilt, Jan Aoertsen van der Bilt.

Vanderbilt married four times and divorced three times. Her husbands were Robert S. Brinkerhoff; Morton G. Clark; Hans Knopf, a noted magazine photographer; and Curtis B. Kellar, a Mobil Oil attorney. Her three sons were Lincoln Gill Clark, Paul Vanderbilt Knopf and Stephen John Knopf.

Her advice is still so valued that a memorial Twitter page, @AmyVSociety, regularly Tweets her ideas.

CORNELIUS VANDERBILT

"Commodore" Cornelius Vanderbilt was a self-made shipping and railroad tycoon born on Staten Island in 1794. In his humble boyhood, he operated a sailboat with his father that carried cargo between Staten Island and Manhattan. He spent a brief time as a steamship captain for a wealthy man, learning the ropes before starting his own business in the 1820s. He would become one of the nation's largest operators of steamships and was either involved in fare wars with other companies or being paid handsomely by them not to compete.

"In the process, the Commodore, as he was publicly nicknamed, gained a reputation for being fiercely competitive and ruthless," according to History.com. "In the 1860s, he shifted his focus to the railroad industry, where he built another empire and helped make railroad transportation more efficient. When Vanderbilt died, he was worth more than $100 million."

During the U.S. Civil War, Cornelius Vanderbilt donated his largest and fastest steamship, named the *Vanderbilt* and built for around $1 million, to the Union navy. The vessel was used to chase down Confederate raiders.

In 1813, Vanderbilt married his cousin Sophia Johnson, and the couple eventually had thirteen children. (A year after his first wife died in 1868, Vanderbilt married another female cousin, Frank Armstrong Crawford, who was more than four decades his junior.)

In the 1840s, Vanderbilt constructed a large brick home for his family at 10 Washington Place, in Manhattan's present-day Greenwich Village neighborhood. Despite his growing wealth, the city's elite residents were slow to accept Vanderbilt, considering him rough and uncultured.

In the early 1850s, during the California Gold Rush, a time before transcontinental railroads, Vanderbilt launched a steamship service that transported prospectors from New York to San Francisco via a route across Nicaragua. His route was faster than an established route across Panama and much speedier than the other alternative, around Cape Horn at the southern tip of South America, which could take months. Vanderbilt's new line was an instant success, earning more than $1 million (about $26 million in today's money) a year.

In the 1860s, Vanderbilt shifted his focus from shipping to the railroad industry, which was entering a period of great expansion. He gained control of a number of railway lines operating between Chicago and New York and established an interregional railroad system. According to T.J. Styles, author of *The First Tycoon: The Epic Life of Cornelius Vanderbilt*, "This was a

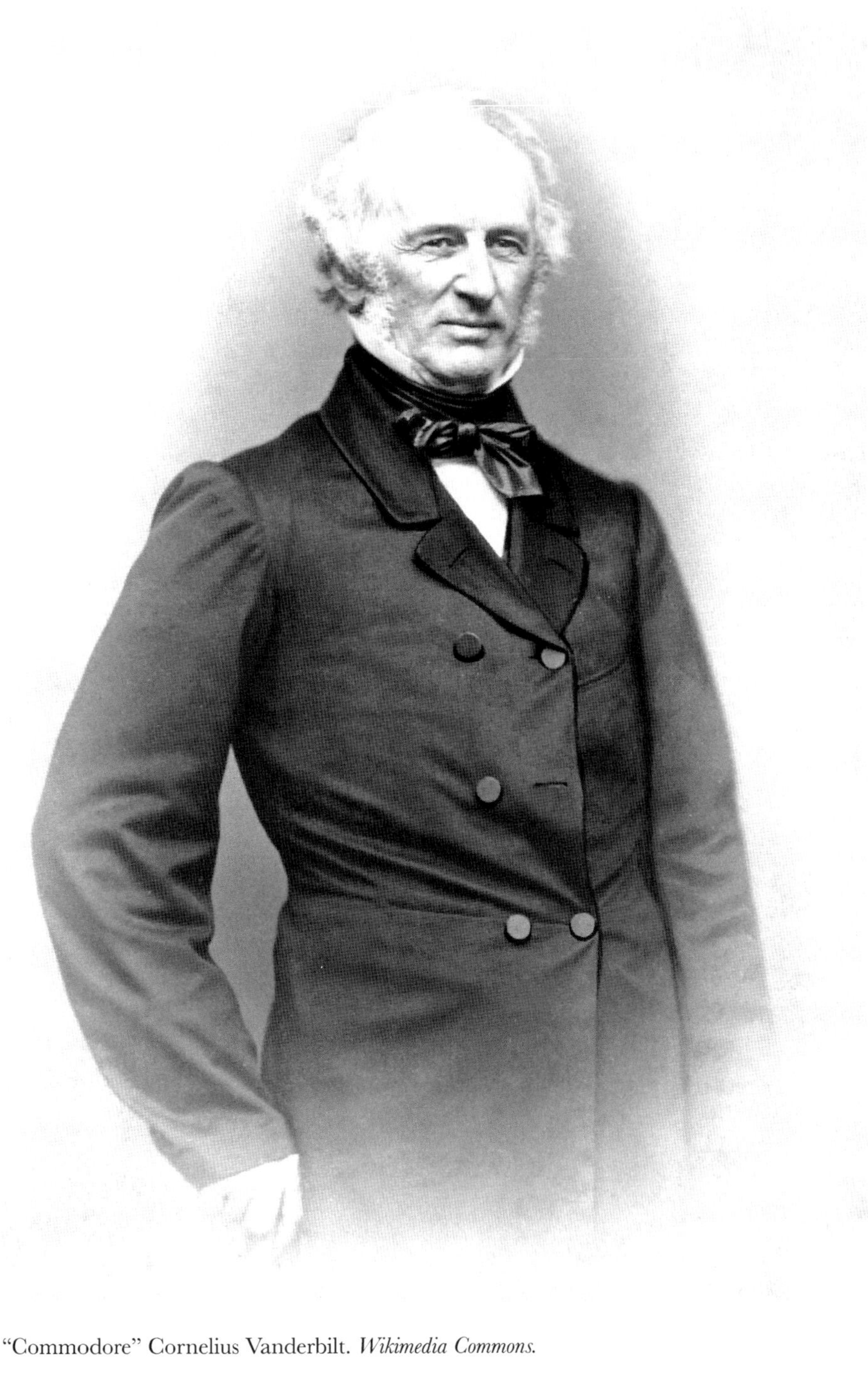

"Commodore" Cornelius Vanderbilt. *Wikimedia Commons.*

major transformation of the railroad network, which previously had been fragmented into numerous short railroads, each with its own procedures, timetables, and rolling stock. The creation of a coherent system spanning several states lowered costs, increased efficiency, and sped up travel and shipment times."

Vanderbilt was the driving force behind the construction of Manhattan's Grand Central Depot, which opened in 1871. The station eventually was torn down and replaced by present-day Grand Central Terminal, which opened in 1913.

Vanderbilt was not known for his philanthropy. The one large gift he made was in 1873, constructing and endowing Vanderbilt University in Nashville, Tennessee, with $1 million.

Marcia Clark

Author Clifford Linedecker wrote in *Marcia Clark: Her Private Trials and Public Triumphs* that famed California-born O.J. Simpson prosecutor Clark "for a time was so sheltered by her religious parents that when she went out she was watched over by a cautiously solicitous female chaperone."

She may have been sheltered, but she was a voracious reader, devouring Nancy Drew and Hardy Boys mysteries and making up some of her own crime stories.

When the Food and Drug Administration (FDA) transferred her chemist father to New York in her teen years, she and her family moved to Queen Street in Staten Island's Manor Heights. Here, Marcia Rachel Kleks, as she was known then, attended Susan Wagner High School, graduating in the new school's first class in 1971. She began dating and even starred in the school's production of *The Man Who Came to Dinner* as the temptress.

Now an author, news consultant and screenwriter, Clark is best known for her role as the lead prosecutor in the O.J. Simpson double murder trial in 1995, in which the former National Football League (NFL) star was accused of killing his ex-wife, Nicole Brown, and her friend Ron Goldman. The trial brought the nation to a halt and dealt with racial divisions previously piqued by the Rodney King case in Los Angeles.

"When I finished writing this book [*Without a Doubt*] in 1997, I couldn't imagine that we would still be talking about the *People v. Orenthal James Simpson* nearly twenty years later. But really, no trial since then has been as heavily covered, as widely followed or as intensely analyzed," she wrote in the foreword for the new edition of the #1 *New York Times* bestseller. "Nor has any other case stirred up such a maelstrom of issues—race, celebrity, domestic violence, and the impact of media coverage on the criminal justice system."

She was also the lead prosecutor previously on the Robert John Bardo murder case involving young actress Rebecca Schaeffer.

Her Amazon author profile states she has written the Rachel Knight and Samantha Brinkman mystery series. The bestselling *Without a Doubt*, which she co-wrote, chronicles her work on the Simpson trial. Clark has been a frequent commentator on a variety of shows and networks, including *Today*, *Good Morning America*, *The Oprah Winfrey Show*, CNN and MSNBC, as well as a legal correspondent for *Entertainment Tonight*.

Chapter 5

The Hilltops and Their History

Similar to how the eternal city of Rome was built on majestic hills, where powerful Roman emperors lived and ruled the land, Staten Island, too, was built on many extravagant, hilly terrains, where some of the most influential people of its early history resided and built their empires.

The historical hills of Staten Island begin from the northeast corner of the Island and continue through to the middle of the region. Some of the wooded hills include the highest peak on the Eastern Seaboard, offering breathtaking views of land and sea. These hundred-year-old hilltops contain some of Staten Island's oldest secrets and hold the key to its intriguing past. Containing some of the wealthiest Staten Island neighborhoods, they are also home to several colleges and universities, private academies, a country club, golf courses, historic landmarks, lighthouses and even a museum.

Todt Hill

According to Douglas Keister's book *Stories in Stone New York: A Field Guide to New York City Cemeteries and Their Residents*, the name of this notable hill is derived from the Dutch language; the Dutch translation of the word *todt* is "dead." Another explanation for its name refers to the rocky terrain and lack of vegetation at its summit. The Moravian Cemetery—one of the Island's oldest (and yet another reference to "dead"), built in 1740—is carved into 113 acres at the foot of the Todt Hill ridge. Many of New York

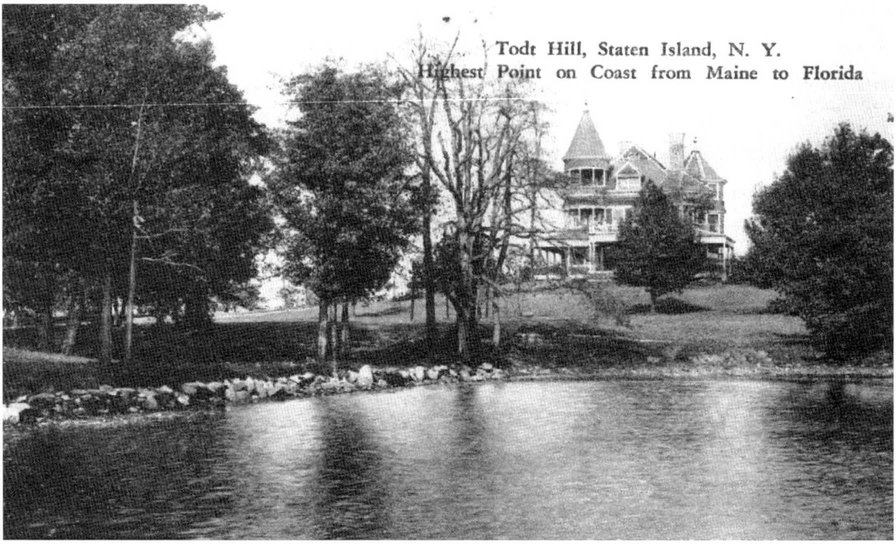

Picturesque view of a Todt Hill mansion and pond. *New York Public Library Digital Collection.*

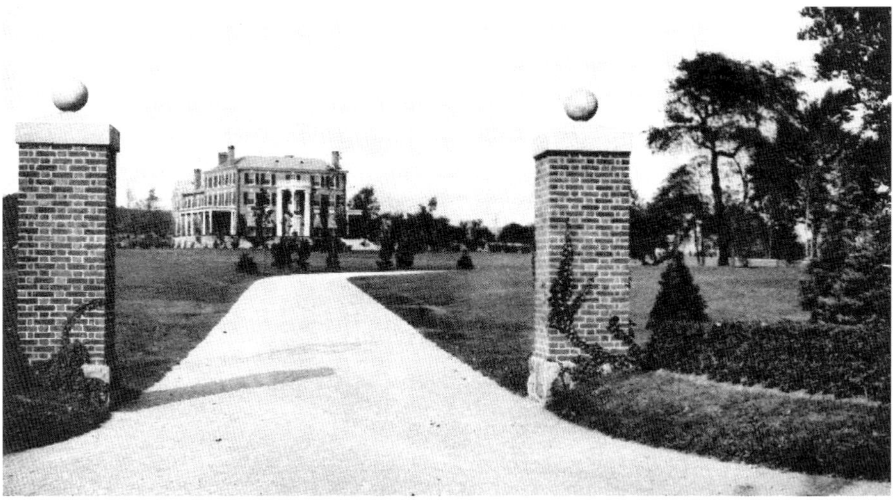

The entrance to the grounds of a large estate on Todt Hill. *New York Public Library Digital Collection.*

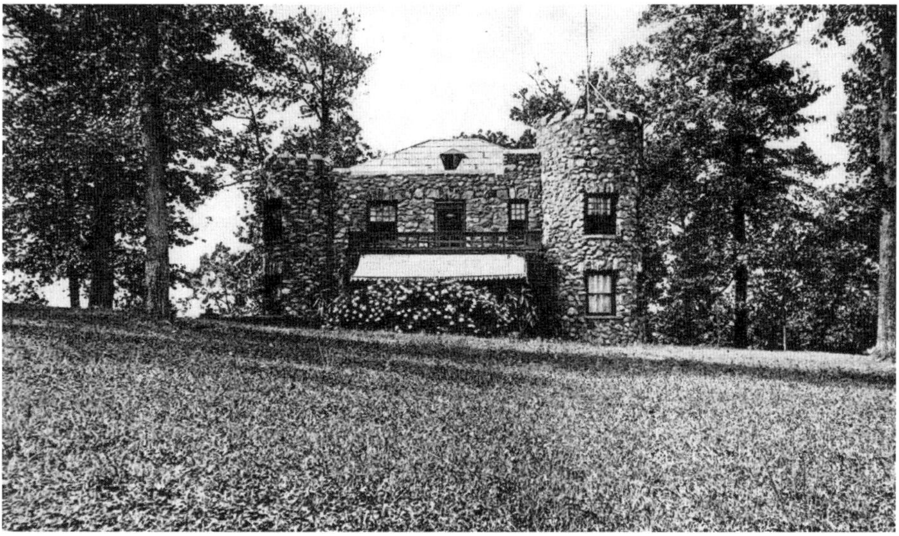

The exterior view of a stone mansion and its property on Todt Hill. *New York Public Library Digital Collection.*

City's most prestigious and influential people are laid to rest here, including illustrious entrepreneurs such as the Vanderbilts and infamous mobster Paul Castellano, head of the Gambino crime family.

Todt Hill predominately comprises serpentine rock and is 400 feet tall, providing the highest elevation on the Eastern Seaboard at 390 feet, according to *Mannahatta: A Natural History of New York City*, by Eric Sanderson. There are also several man-made lakes, preserved wooded areas and natural ponds full of wildlife. It maintains its mystique and allure by being both quiet and reserved. Todt Hill is most known as being one of the most prestigious communities on Staten Island. With an abundance of lavish estates and mansions depicting all styles of architectural design that are neatly tucked into the plateaus and cliffs of each winding road, it remains one of the most desirable neighborhoods money can buy.

Many of the homes built in the early twentieth century were designed by renowned architect Ernest Flagg, and today, a street on Todt Hill bears his name in his honor. Beyond their ornate entrance gates, these stunning estates are privy to the most beautiful views of the ocean, bridges and beautiful treetops for miles on end.

Staten Island Academy, the St. Francis Center for Spirituality and the Richmond County Country Club and its manicured golf course are also nestled in this secluded hill. With its extensive landscapes, unparalleled views and privacy, it's no wonder professional baseball players, surgeons, television stars, financiers, artists and even notorious mobsters call Todt Hill their home.

WARD HILL

This stately hill offers large homes with spectacular views of New York City and its skyline. The homes that are carefully woven within an abundance of trees reflect the styles of a bygone era. Many residences have old-world charm and character with wraparound porches, stunning landscaped grounds and breathtaking views. They symbolize the power and the wealth of the nineteenth century in its heyday.

At one time, Ward Hill was known to be the area where many in the Staten Island political echelon lived. Ward Hill was named for Caleb T. Ward, who, according to the 2009 National Register of Historic Places, National Park Service, purchased the property situated at the summit of the hill. Today, his home is a New York City landmark.

LIGHTHOUSE HILL

This hilltop neighborhood, like many of the others, is noted for having some of the most opulent homes on the Island. Each home is unique, both in design and how it is built into the mountainous curves. Many homes are gamble-roofed structures and reflect the Federal style, while others are splendid contemporary estates. The area is full of private winding roads, with aged oak, maple and birch trees lining its pathways. Lighthouse Hill is lavish, serene and very private, offering homeowners outstanding views of Historic Richmond Town and the New York Harbor. The hill is surrounded by the Staten Island Greenbelt, which comprises hiking trails and is adjacent to La Tourette Golf Course. At La Tourette Golf Course, what serves as the clubhouse today was at one time a farmhouse built in 1836. It is considered a landmark and in 1982 was added to the National Register of Historic Places. In the 1800s, Lighthouse Hill was predominately farmlands and pastures owned by wealthy residents.

Lighthouse Hill was originally referred to as Richmond Hill, as referenced in K.T. Jackson's *Encyclopedia of New York*. Furthermore, it is also home to the

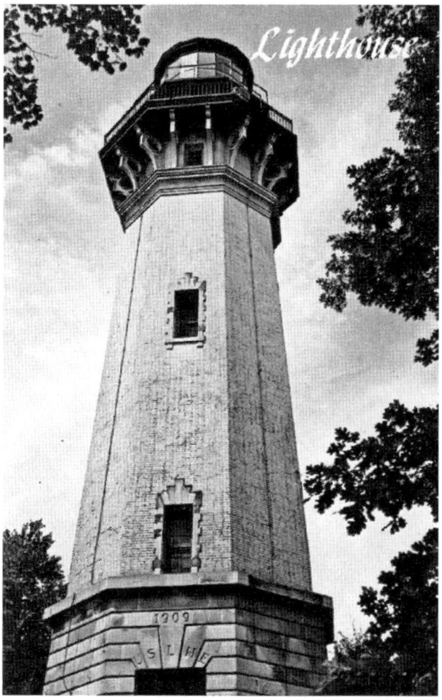

The Staten Island Range Light, Lighthouse Hill. *New York Public Library Digital Collection.*

ninety-foot-tall Staten Island Range Light Lighthouse, built in 1912. After the addition of the Staten Island Range Light Lighthouse, it is mentioned in E. Willensky and N. White's book *AIA Guide to New York City*, the hill adopted its new name, Lighthouse Hill.

Also, Lighthouse Hill is home to the beautiful Jacques Marchais Museum of Tibetan Art. The museum, built in 1947, is listed in the National Register of Historic Places. Designed to reflect a Himalayan monastery, its unique architecture and grounds accent the distinctive beauty of its environment with inviting terraces, tropical gardens and ponds for visitors to enjoy.

In another point of interest, world-famous architect Frank Lloyd Wright designed the only residential structure in New York City on Lighthouse Hill. The William and Catherine Cass House, also known as the "Crimson Beech," was constructed in 1958. It is nestled in an enclave of trees and in 1990 was declared a landmark.

EMERSON HILL

Bordering the south side of Todt Hill, old cobblestone entrance gates welcome homeowners into the affluent neighborhood of Emerson Hill. With homes rich in design, with copper roofs and carriage houses, this neighborhood's views are boundless. The many farms and estates of the twentieth century were owned by wealthy shipping magnates and prominent landowners.

According to author Henry Seidel Canby in *Thoreau*, the hill is named for Judge William Emerson, brother of the famed poet-philosopher Ralph Waldo Emerson. Judge William Emerson lived in his home, which he named the Snuggery, with his family. Ralph Waldo Emerson and fellow friend and philosopher Henry David Thoreau would frequent Staten Island during the

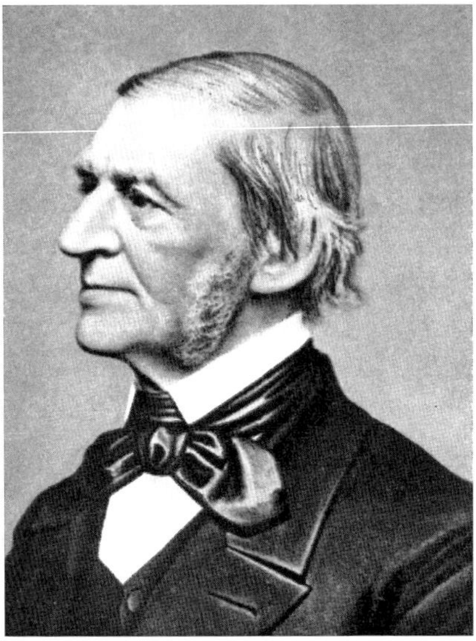

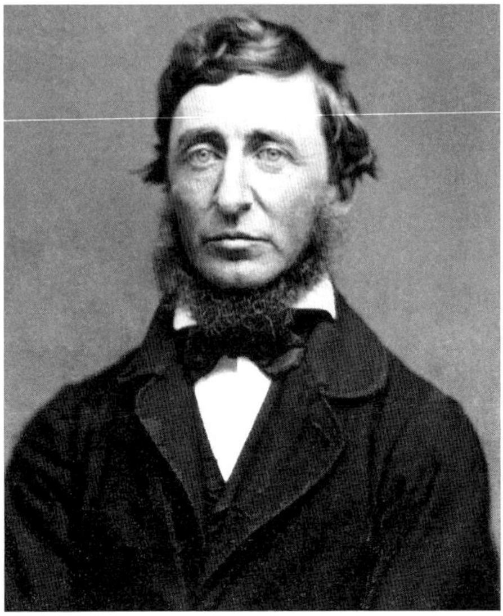

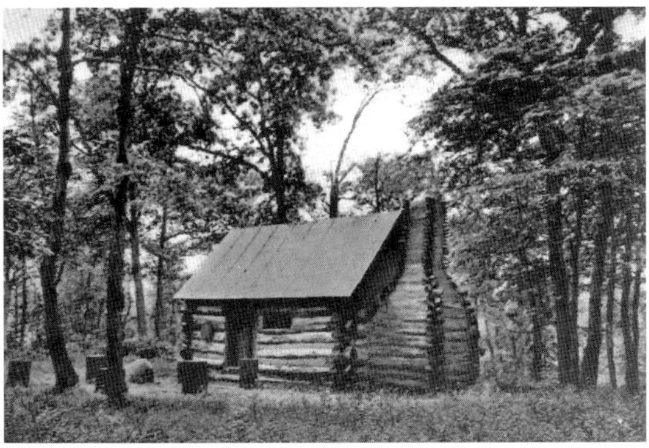

Above, left: A portrait of philosopher and poet Ralph Waldo Emerson. *New York Public Library Digital Collection.*

Above, right: A portrait of philosopher and poet Henry David Thoreau. *Wikimedia Commons.*

Left: The cabin on Emerson Hill known as "The Philosopher's Retreat." *New York Public Library Digital Collection.*

summer months for holiday. During this time, it is said Thoreau would be employed as a tutor for Judge Emerson's children.

Interestingly enough, Kathryn Carse mentions in her 2009 article "Log-Cabin Retreat Once Stood on Emerson Hill" in the *Staten Island Advance* that real estate developer Cornelius G. Kolff owned a great deal of property on Emerson Hill, and in respect and honor of the Emerson brothers and their contribution to Staten Island, he named the hill after them. In 1910, Kolff built a log cabin retreat on Emerson Hill. The cabin, surrounded by chestnut trees, was known to become a haven for the great thinkers of that era. The cabin, aptly named the "Philosopher's Retreat," served as a meeting place for philosophers, politicians and businessmen alike. Comprising a fireplace with logs set in front of it for sitting, the cabin was where men met, smoked pipes and shared their viewpoints of life.

Today, Emerson Hill is distinctive in its cottage stone styles, winding streets and exceptional views of New York Harbor and the Verrazano Bridge. Opulent homes, some dating back to the early 1900s, quietly hide under the canopy of statuesque trees.

Grymes Hill

This majestic hill offers the second-highest elevation on Staten Island. Towering above the valley with an elevation of 310 feet, its heavenly views of the land below and of the waterfront are unsurpassed, making this a very sought-after community to reside in. Its roads bend within the hills and ensure privacy at every turn. The home styles vary between Renaissance estates, palatial Tudors and contemporary mansions, many of which belonged to business tycoons. There are also several hundred garden apartments present, developed in the late 1940s by real estate mogul Fred Trump, father of President Donald Trump.

Hero Park, a two-acre parcel of land, was donated in 1920 by Dr. and Mrs. Louis A. Dreyfus as a gift to the public. The park is adorned with blossoming trees, flowering gardens and wrought-iron benches, as referenced in Jerry Cheslow's 1989 article "If You're Thinking of Living in: Grymes Hill" in the *New York Times*. The homes in this neighborhood are considered to be some of the most expensive on the Island.

Grymes Hill is named after Suzette Grymes, the widow of the first governor of Louisiana, William Claiborne. After her husband's death in 1817, Suzette married reputable New Orleans attorney John R. Grymes and, according to author Claire Wilson in her 2006 article "Developed Enough as It Is, Thanks" in the *New York Times*, settled on Staten Island in 1836. Grymes owned a tremendous portion of the hilly landscape.

The hill comprises predominately serpentine rock, and at one time its main road was called Serpentine Road. In his book *History and Legend of Howard Avenue and the Serpentine Road, Grymes Hill, Staten Island*, author Charles Hine says the name of Serpentine Road was changed to Howard Avenue in honor of Major Charles Howard, a prominent real estate developer who constructed many of the homes on the hill.

Additionally, beer production was quite popular. During the mid-1800s, caves were strategically carved into the hill to produce beer and operate

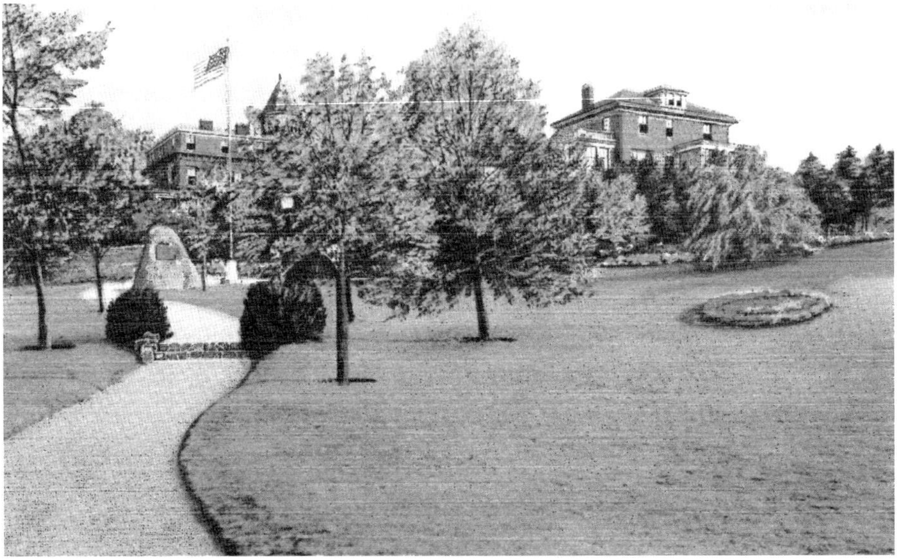

A postcard depicting Hero Park on Grymes Hill. *New York Public Library Digital Collection.*

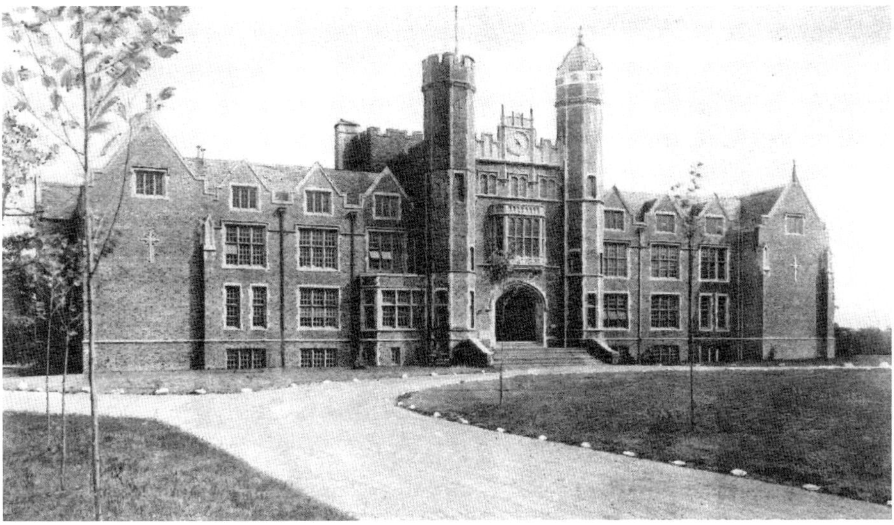

Wagner College, Grymes Hill, Staten Island, New York, circa early 1900s. *New York Public Library Digital Collection.*

as breweries, as mentioned in Patricia Salmon's 2012 article "Staten Island Memories: The Business of Brewing" in the *Staten Island Advance*.

Grymes Hill is also the location of several educational institutions. The 16 acres of property once owned by Notre Dame College for Women is now home to St. John's University. Wagner College encompasses 110 acres of pristine land and was formerly the home of Augustinian Academy, a Roman Catholic high school named after the monks who oversaw it. Notre Dame High School, a private female high school, is located in the center of the hilly region. Woodland Cemetery and Silver Lake Cemetery lie at the foot of the hill.

With breathtaking views of the Island and the Verrazano Bridge, the 1920s former home of prominent businessman and silk importer Louis A. Stirn and his wife, Laura, is today known as Casa Belvedere. Casa Belvedere, Staten Island's Italian Cultural Center, is a vibrant hub of Italian culture, tradition and language. It offers the public classes in Italian cooking, Italian language and educational lectures in Italian culture. It also hosts bocce ball tournaments and fundraising events. The structure was designated a New York City landmark in 2001 and was listed in the National Register of Historic Places in 2010.

Chapter 6

Staten Island

The Perfect Hideout for Revolutionaries

Governor Lajos Kossuth of Hungary

Governor Lajos (Louis) Kossuth, the Hungarian independence fighter, arrived in America on December 4, 1851, after an enthusiastic reception in England. His steamer the *Humboldt* docked at the Quarantine on Staten Island in what is now St. George. He would stay for a year, first in the home of Dr. Doane and next in Nautilus Hall, on land owned by Governor Daniel D. Tompkins here.

According to *Governor Louis Kossuth With His Public Speeches in the United States and a Brief History of the Hungarian War of Independence*, published shortly thereafter at 128 Nassau Street, "Kossuth Fever," as it was already known in England, quickly ignited Staten Island. "As soon as her [the ship's] arrival was announced, the forts and batteries fired a salute of thirty-one guns—one for each of the States of the Union. Their echoes awakened the island, and brought thousands of people to the shore."

Greeted by local dignitaries, Kossuth was reportedly moved by their warmth and sincerity. He said:

> *Thanks for your generous sentiments, expressed in such generous words!... But do not speak of your nation as an infant—oh no! She is a giant and in less than seventy years has grown to the stature which the older nations have not reached in a thousand. The genius of your Fulton has blotted out the distance across the Atlantic, and may the generous confidence of the young*

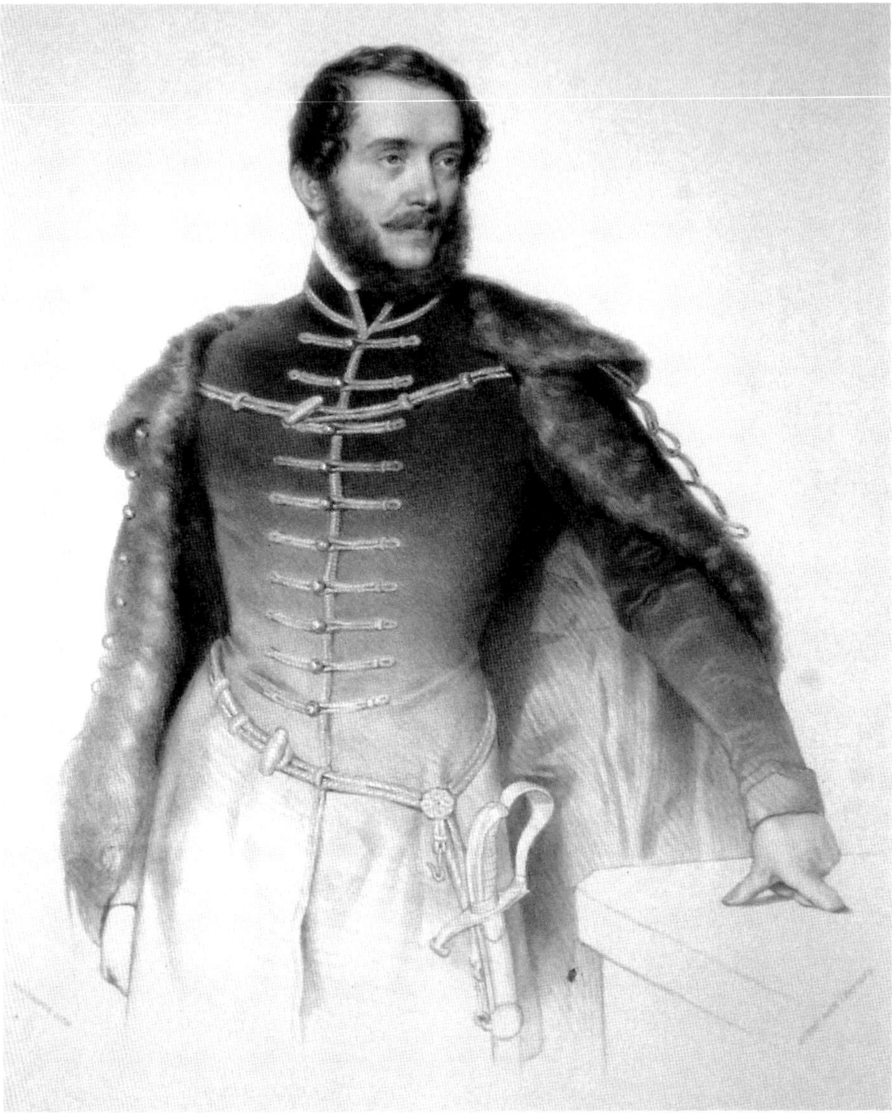

Governor Lajos Kossuth, Hungarian revolutionary. *Wikimedia Commons.*

giant know no distance when I ask a fraternal hand for old Europe.... May your kind anticipations of me be not disappointed. I am a plain man. I have nothing in me but an honest fidelity to those principles which have made you great, and my most ardent wish is that my own country may be, if not great as yours, at least as free and as happy, which it will be in the

> *establishment of the same great principles. The sounds I now hear* [there were cannons and shouts from the shore] *seem to me the trumpet of resurrection for down-trodden humanity throughout the world.*

The next day at dawn, European revolutionary flags were unfurled at the Quarantine and there was a twenty-one-gun salute. A vast assemblage of people on Staten Island got underway at noon.

Kossuth spoke again: "Citizens, be, therefore, fervently thanked for your generous welcome to me on my arrival to your happy shores. Be both thanked and blessed for the sanction of my hopes which you have addressed."

The legendary figure returned to Europe the following year and started unsuccessful uprisings in Hungary in 1865 and 1866. He died in Italy in 1894 without seeing freedom for the Hungarian people.

JEREMIAH O'DONOVAN ROSSA OF IRELAND

Legendary Irish nationalist and revolutionary Jeremiah O'Donovan Rossa lived for many years in exile in the Mariners Harbor section of Staten Island with his family, publishing resistance newspapers and continuing his cause among sympathizers around the city. The controversial character is sometimes referred to as "the first terrorist," given his penchant for using dynamite.

He was born in September 1831 in Reenascreena, County Cork, and was the child of a tenant farmer. "As a young man he came to believe his family were descendants of an ancient Gaelic clan who ruled the area before their lands were confiscated and planted by the English in the 17th century," according to the journal *Politics* in Ireland.

O'Donovan Rossa worked for a time as a shopkeeper in Skibbereen, where he began to socialize with Irish nationalists and revolutionaries. When his family suffered during the Great Famine in 1847, he was further radicalized. He married three times and had eighteen children.

He became part of the Irish Republican Brotherhood, also known as the Fenians, which was founded in 1858 in Dublin. "O'Donovan Rossa was arrested and imprisoned without trial between December 1858 and July 1859. Accused of plotting a Fenian uprising in 1865 and served his time in Pentonville, Portland and Chatham prisons in England during which he was held in solitary confinement on bread and water and prohibited from corresponding with his associates," according to www.

politics.ie. "Nonetheless he was elected as an MP for Tipperary in 1869 by election."

He was granted amnesty in 1870 and made his way to America, settling on Staten Island. He traveled with four other revolutionaries: John Devoy, Charles Underwood O'Connell, Henry (Harry) Mulleda and John McClure. Together, they were given the infamous nickname the "Cuba Five" because they sailed the SS *Cuba* to America.

Here in New York City, O'Donovan Rossa became active almost immediately, joining the Clan Na Gael movement. Soon, he founded the *United Irishman* newspaper, which raised money for his cause.

In the 1880s, he headed the Dynamite Campaign, a group of bombings on government facilities in the United Kingdom. "Scores of people were injured especially during a series of attacks on the London Underground and during one attack on London Bridge three IRB members were blown up by their own bomb," according to the political journal.

After O'Donovan Rossa's passing, his body was repatriated to Dublin for propaganda purposes, and the eulogy given by fellow Fenian Padraig Pearse set off the Easter Rising of 1916, which resulted in the independence of the Republic of Ireland.

According to the journal *Stair na hÉireann* (History of Ireland):

> *On his deathbed at age 83, Jeremiah O'Donovan Rossa sent for his old friends, John Devoy and Richard O'Sullivan Burke. He died a tired old warrior on 29 June 1915 in St Vincent's Hospital on Staten Island, New York after a two year illness. Devoy, aware that when Young Irelander Terrence Bellew McManus had died in San Francisco in 1866 the funeral procession became a massive propaganda coup, he contacted Tom Clarke in Ireland, himself a Clan na Gael member, and Rossa's remains were sent home.*

He was given a huge welcome in what turned out to be one of the largest funerals in Irish history, the journal states.

> *In a remarkable scene, the road outside the cemetery was lined with spectators, as for several hours beforehand crowds had been assembling at the cemetery in anticipation of seeing O'Donovan Rossa being finally laid to rest; garnering substantial publicity for the Irish Volunteers.... Standing over the grave, giving the graveside oration was, Pádraig Pearse, which remains one of the most famous speeches of the Irish independence movement stirring his audience to a call to arms. It ended with the lines:*

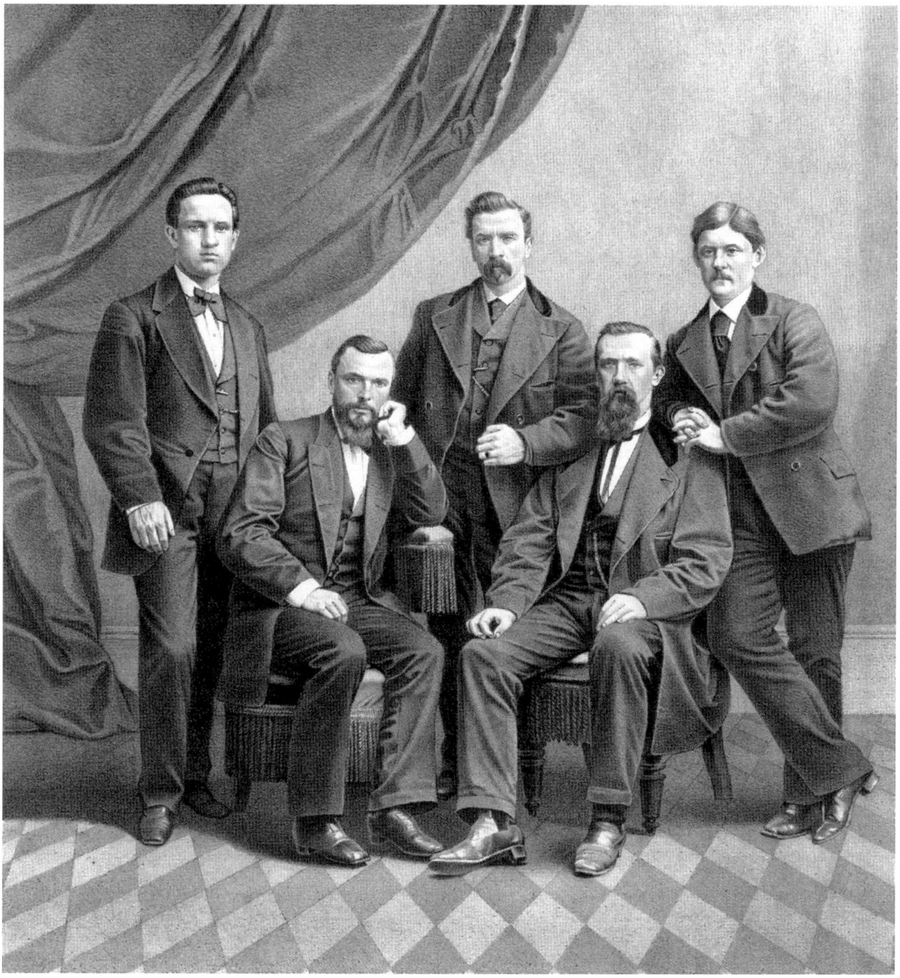

Irish revolutionary Jeremiah O'Donovan Rossa (*seated, right*). *Wikimedia Commons*.

> *"They think that they have pacified Ireland. They think that they have purchased half of us and intimidated the other half. They think that they have foreseen everything, think that they have provided against everything; but, the fools, the fools, the fools!—They have left us our Fenian dead, and while Ireland holds these graves, Ireland unfree shall never be at peace."*

Several generations of O'Donovan Rossa's descendants remained on Staten Island, among them the late New York City councilman Jerome X. O'Donovan.

AARON BURR

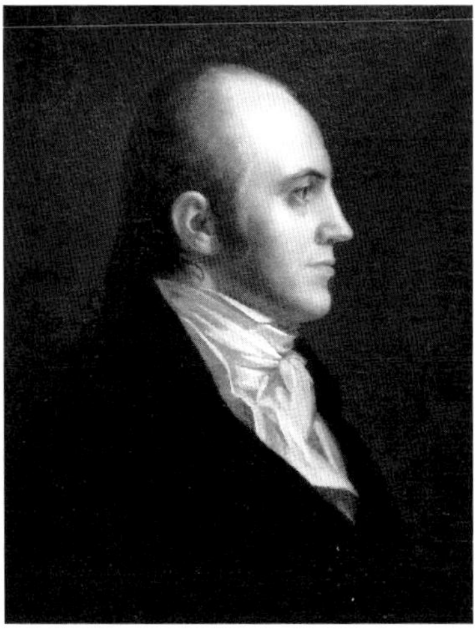

Vice president of the United States Aaron Burr, who killed Alexander Hamilton in a duel. *Wikimedia Commons.*

Aaron Burr spent his final days under the care of a prominent cousin, Judge Ogden Edwards, at the former Hotel St. James in Port Richmond on Staten Island. He had suffered a series of strokes, leaving him partially paralyzed. He died here on September 14, 1836.

And he spent some of his earliest days here as well. According to the Aaron Burr Association, he ran away from home when he was ten and took the ferry to Staten Island. He then got a job on a ship as a cabin boy, but his uncle Timothy came to fetch him. "Although Timothy was strict," the association website explains, "he and Aaron had a good relationship. Ten years after the war, when Timothy went bankrupt nephew Aaron satisfied his guardian's creditors at ten shillings on the pound."

He tried to return to the Island from Valley Forge in 1777, planning a march against the British posts here, as he knew the territory. "He asked Washington for 200 men of his own regiment, but Washington gave the expedition to Lord Stirling and the Marquis de Lafayette," his association recounts. "Lafayette asked Washington if Hamilton could lead a battalion, but Washington refused that, too, saying he could not afford to give up Hamilton."

His ties here would continue. In 1801, Hamilton served as the attorney preparing the will for Robert Randall, setting up a retirement home for merchant mariners that would become the iconic Sailors' Snug Harbor, now a cultural center.

Aaron Burr is most famous for the duel on July 11, 1804, in which he shot and killed Alexander Hamilton in nearby Weehawken, New Jersey. Burr had been on a collision course with his rival since 1791. According to Bio.com, that year, Burr was victorious over General Philip Schuyler, Hamilton's father-in-law, in a Senate race. He served for seven years, during which the rivalry was palpable. When Burr subsequently lost to Schuyler in a reelection, he blamed Hamilton for hurting his reputation in campaigning against him.

When, in 1800, Burr faced off for the U.S. presidency with Thomas Jefferson, they each received the same number of electoral votes. Members of the House of Representatives were left to pick the winner. When the House met to discuss the election, Burr's rival, Hamilton, vocalized his support for Jefferson and his disapproval of Burr. In the end, Jefferson won the presidency and Burr became vice president. Burr was furious, believing that Hamilton had manipulated the vote in Jefferson's favor.

Four years later, he was completing his run as vice president and decided to run to be New York's governor. When he lost that election, he blamed Hamilton again for ruining his reputation and challenged him to a duel. The famous confrontation happened on the morning of July 11, 1804. Burr shot Hamilton to death. The public outcry was such that Burr had to leave New York and New Jersey, but he did return to the nation's capital to complete his term. He was never prosecuted.

SANTA ANNA OF MEXICO

The self-described "Napolean of the West," General Antonio Lopez de Santa Anna ruled Mexico as president six times in periods of great unrest.

He famously led the battle of the Alamo in 1836 near San Antonio, Texas. There, 1,500 Mexicans annihilated just 200 American soldiers, including Davy Crockett and Jim Bowie. "Remember the Alamo!" is a rallying cry remembered even today.

Some twenty years after that infamous battle, he was welcomed to Staten Island by Governor Daniel Tompkins, whom he had previously hosted in luxurious style on a visit to Mexico. Santa Anna lived in the borough for a decade from 1865 to 1875, making plans to return to power (which were never successful) and playing a role in the start of the chewing gum industry.

Here he came to know the inventor Thomas Adams. Adams was intrigued by the field rations still carried by the general—among them, chicle, or gum from the sapodilla tree, which Mexican soldiers chewed in the field. Ultimately, Adams would flavor them, roll them into little balls and sell them at local pharmacies, citing health benefits like improved digestion and stress reduction. Sales grew such that he opened a factory for the sweets in New Jersey and later on Staten Island itself. Adams Chewing Gum was born, and an industry that today is valued at $19 billion followed.

According to History.com, Santa Anna once staged a funeral for his amputated leg:

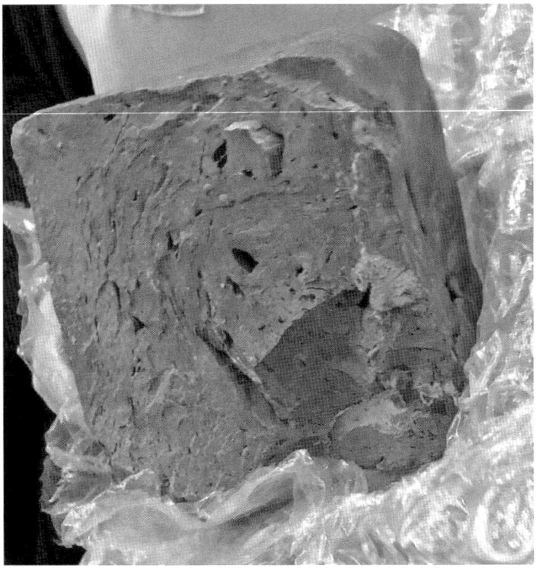

Mexican General Santa Anna brought this block of chicle with him to America, helping to start the bubblegum industry. *Author's collection.*

> *Two years after the 1836 Battle of the Alamo, Santa Anna led a makeshift army against French forces who had invaded Veracruz, Mexico, in what has been called the Pastry War. After the general was severely wounded by grapeshot fired from a French cannon, doctors were forced to amputate his leg, which Santa Anna buried at his Veracruz hacienda. After he once again assumed the presidency in 1842, Santa Anna exhumed his shriveled leg, paraded it to Mexico City in an ornate coach and buried it beneath a cemetery monument in an elaborate state funeral that included cannon salvos, poetry and lofty orations. Santa Anna's severed leg did not remain in the ground for long, however. In 1844, public opinion turned on the president, and rioters tore down his statues and dug up his leg. A mob tied the severed appendage to a rope and dragged it through the streets of Mexico City while shouting, "Death to the cripple!"*

Santa Anna moved to Mexico City from Staten Island to write his memoir and died a year later. In his autobiography, *The Eagle*, the former general painted himself as a simple man with the best interests of his people at heart, not as the tyrant in the way others described him.

His biographer Will Fowler wrote in *Santa Anna of Mexico*, "He was courageous and he risked his life for his country....He was also notoriously corrupt and amassed a formidable fortune at the height of his career by lining his pockets with government funds. He was charismatic and charming. He was also forceful and ruthless." Fowler concludes that he was an intelligent and contradictory man.

The San Jacinto Museum describes him this way: "While eccentric and arrogant...Santa Anna was nothing if not astute. His heavy-handed tactics in the Texas Revolution were a function of his training. And his political shifts showed his mastery of reading the political tea leaves rather than a penchant for disloyalty."

Chapter 7

Notable Mansions and Landmarks

Some of Staten Island's most compelling and fascinating stories are embedded in its historical landmarks and elaborate mansions. With such a colorful palette depicting everything from the American Revolution and the colonial era to spooky ghost tales, the Island's rich history is riveting. In vignettes highlighting the historical roots of a few of Staten Island's most prominent mansions and renowned landmark sites, one realizes how much of an impact their existence makes in assembling the puzzle pieces of the Island's history.

The Conference House

In the 1600s, England had become quite the dominant force in New America, acquiring for the English colony the New Netherland territory and Staten Island. The English government divided Staten Island into large parcels of land. Governors, lords and distinguished men were the recipients of large allotments of property on which they built their palatial manors.

According to author James C. Connelly in "How New York Acquired Staten Island," from *Proceedings of the New Jersey Historical Society*, a myth references exactly how Staten Island became part of the New York territory rather than belonging to its very close neighbor, the state of New Jersey. The legend is the story of British Royal Navy captain Christopher Billopp (note: his surname has been noted as having many

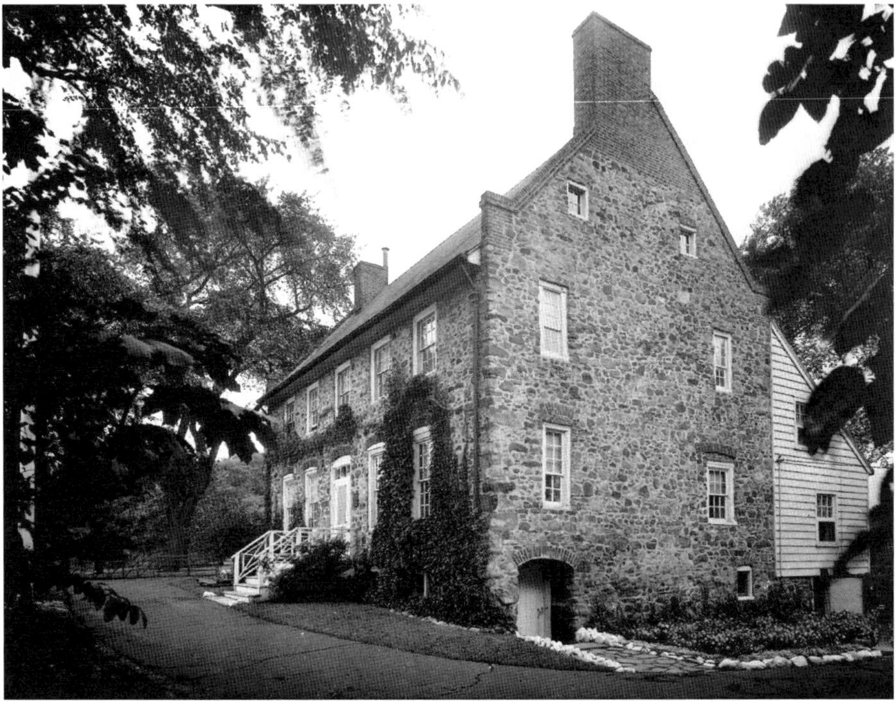

The front exterior of the Conference House. *Library of Congress.*

spelled variations), seafaring skills and a bet. The challenge was that if he could sail completely around Staten Island in one day, then the Island would belong to the colony of New York; if he couldn't accomplish this goal, the Island would belong to New Jersey. Obviously, Captain Billopp circumnavigated the Island successfully; thus, it became a part of New York State. In the mid-1600s, in reward for many years of his loyal service to the Royal Navy, Captain Christopher Billopp was bestowed many acres located on the southernmost tip of Staten Island.

Prior to its European settlement, the specific area given to Billopp by the English was once associated with the Lenape Indians. This Native American tribe traveled along the eastern coastal areas from New York Harbor to the Delaware River. The rural lands were used for hunting deer, foxes and wolves, and the waterways were abundant in fish and oysters. Rossville Points, a recognized design of Native American arrowheads, have been found in multiple locations on the Island, and in fact, the town name Rossville hails from its arrowhead ancestry. These artifacts, along with others indicative of Native Americans and specifically the Lenape Indian tribe, have been noted in the *Anthropological Papers of the American Museum of Natural History* by the American Museum of Natural History. As mentioned in *History of Richmond County (Staten Island), New York*, the Lenape Native American tribe also used some of this land as a burial ground, which is situated on a bluff jutting into Raritan Bay. George H. Pepper of the American Museum of Natural History conducted archaeological digs on the grounds and discovered the decayed bodies of the tribe. Today, this burial area is known as Burial Ridge.

By 1687, Captain Billopp's expansive property encompassed 1,600 acres, which included farms and a two-story manor house made of fieldstone known as the Manor of Bentley, as noted in "Conference House Park, Conference House," New York City Department of Parks and Recreation. The manor was passed down through the generations in the Billopp family and eventually bequeathed to his great-grandson and namesake, Christopher Billopp. A colonel in the British army during the American Revolution, Billopp entertained fellow soldiers at the manor often. In fact, the Island was predominantly occupied by British Loyalists and had headquarters in many Staten Island neighborhoods. According to the "Conference (Billopp) House," National Register of Historic Places, there were several altercations on Staten Island between the British Loyalists and the Patriots during the American Revolution. Billopp, being a commander for the British army, was captured on two separate occasions. Amid battles and turmoil, the Billopp House was designated as the location of a peace conference to be held on September 11, 1776. The peace conference attendees were British Lord Admiral Richard Howe, the commander in chief of British forces in America; and Edward Rutledge, John Adams and Benjamin Franklin, representatives of the Continental Congress. At the time of the conference, England had substantial control over Staten Island, Long Island and New York City, and defeating the Americans seemed to be in their favor. The peace conference (which took place shortly after the signing of the Declaration of Independence) was intended to bring an end to the American Revolution. Lord Howe wanted the Patriots to surrender and return to British control. The Americans disagreed and declined the offer. This ultimately led to seven more years of war and conflict. The Billopp House, where the now-infamous peace conference was held, became known as the Conference House.

Billopp's Point proved ideal for water access to the Revolutionary camps stationed on the New Jersey side. As a result of this strategic military locale, Billopp's Point played a pivotal role on Staten Island for the British army. One such raid, held on October 25, 1779, called "Simcoe's Raid," departed from Billopp's Point. *A History of the Operations of a Partisan Corps Called the*

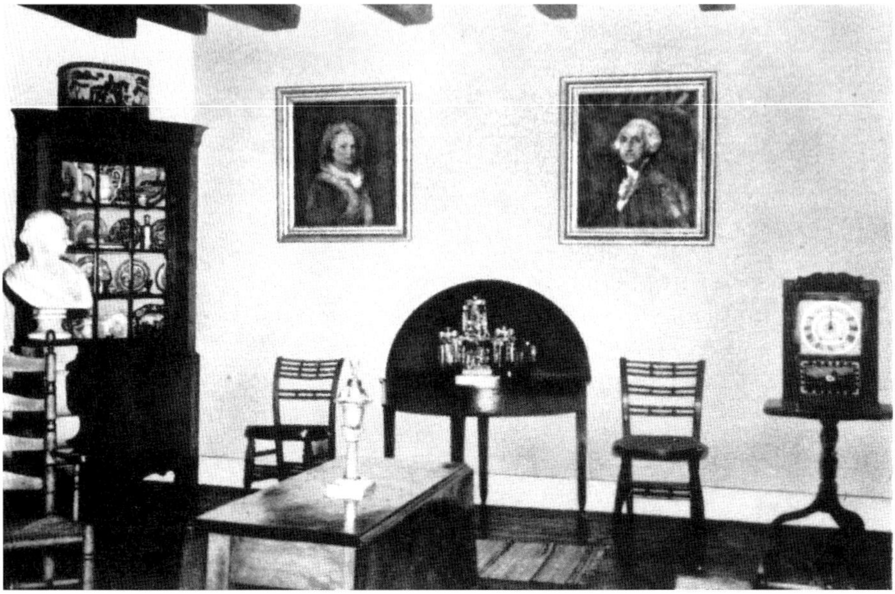

An interior of one of the rooms inside the Conference House, 1668. *New York Public Library Collection.*

Queen's Rangers, a military journal, was written after the war by Queen's Ranger lieutenant John Graves Simcoe. An excerpt of his military journal reads, "The bateaux, and boats, which were appointed to be at Billopp's-point, so as to pass the whole over by twelve o'clock at night, did not arrive till three o'clock in the morning."

Another reference to Billopp's Point as a military meeting point is documented in *Major Andre's Journal* with an entry that reads: "October 25—The Regiments at Amboy received Orders to strike their tents and send them with their baggage to the water's side. Those at Staten Island had orders to leave theirs standing, and repair by 8 o'clock in the evening to Billopp's Point."

Prior to the end of the war, Billopp had sold half of his 1,600 acres and his manor house to Samuel Ward, a farmer. After American independence was won, the remainder of the property was confiscated and eventually became the property of the City of New York. The house had been abandoned, and the nonprofit organization the Conference House Association was formed, according to the 1901 *New York Times* article "A Bill for the Preservation of the Historic Mansion. Continental Congress Committee There Rejected Lord Howe's Offer of Amnesty." Additionally, the 1926 article "City Will

Preserve Old Billopp House, Landmark at Tottenville, S.I., Was Scene of Peace Conference in '76. Given by Realty Co." discussed the preservation of the Conference House and its historical importance. The Conference House Park was created in 1926, and the Conference House was declared a National Historic Landmark in 1966.

There are plenty of ghost stories swirling around the Billopp House and its property, which are said to be the location of the most haunted sightings on Staten Island. Many horrifying legends surround Billopp himself. According to an eerie legendary tale, Billopp murdered one of his maids, whom he believed to be a spy for the Patriots. According to hauntedstatenisland.com, the ghost of the maid haunts the house with flickering candlelight in the windows at night. Another tale speaks of how Billopp left his fiancée, and she died of a broken heart, with her shrieking wails of sadness often heard billowing through the house. Other spooky tales surround the property itself, where the grounds are supposedly haunted by British soldiers marching through the escape tunnels buried under the home. Other sightings have been said to be Native American spirits hovering over their ancient burial grounds.

Today, the Conference House Park finds its home set in the picturesque and peaceful area known as Tottenville. With incomparable views of New

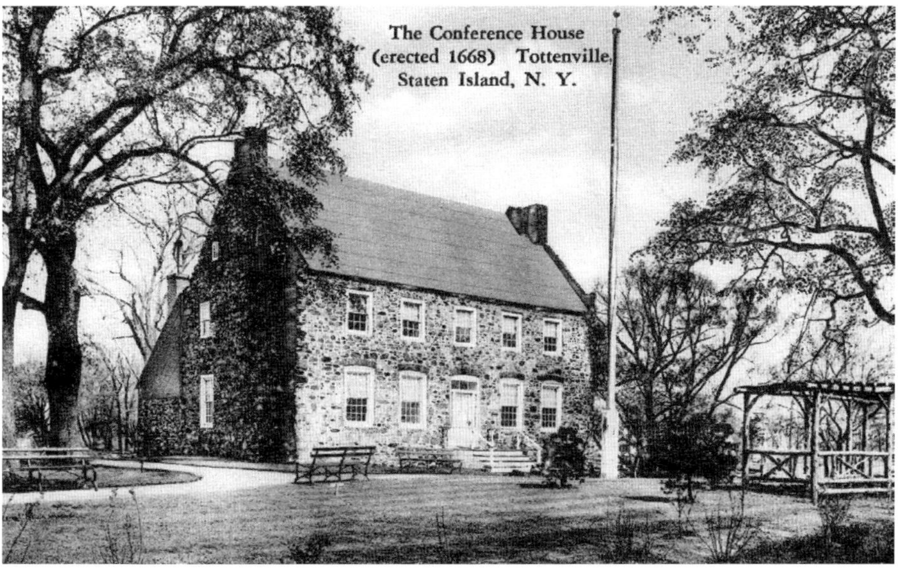

Front exterior of the Conference House. *New York Public Library Collection.*

Jersey and the waterfront, it is home to picnic pavilions, and hiking and biking trails spread across three acres of land. The park, which sits at the southernmost point of Staten Island, offers reenactments of colonial days, educational exhibits, tours of several historic homes on its grounds and ghost tours too.

THE ALICE AUSTEN HOUSE

Alice Austen (1866–1952) was a female pioneer in the field of photography. She leaves behind a legacy of eight thousand photographs that depict her independent lifestyle, points of interest and personal travels. Most of her photographs were inspired by the loves of her life: her family, friends and home. She is also known for capturing poignant images reflecting the daily life and strife of New York City immigrants. Her story is both beautiful and tragic.

Born Elizabeth Alice Munn in March 1866, she was abandoned by her father as a baby. Left with neither income nor a way to provide for her child, her mother relocated to Staten Island, and they moved in with her wealthy family. She would become the only child in her family to live with her grandparents, aunts and uncles in a home they referred to as Clear Comfort. According to "Alice Austen House," National Park Service, she dropped the surname Munn and was called Alice Austen, initialing all her photographic negatives with "EAA" for Elizabeth Alice Austen. As mentioned in Claire Wilson's 2006 article "A Quiet Slice of New York Waterfront" in the *New York Times*, Alice grew up in an eighteenth-century farmhouse in the Rosebank neighborhood of Staten Island, and it would be here where she would spend her formative years with her rather wealthy family. It was at Clear Comfort that she was introduced to photography as a child. Her uncle Oswald Muller, a prominent shipping magnate, brought home a large, cumbersome camera from one of his many voyages overseas and allowed her to use it. Her intrigue and intelligence quickly transformed her newfound hobby into what would become her lifelong passion. Observing her agility and patience with the camera, her uncle allowed her to use it in his absence. Alice diligently documented the meticulous gardens and landscapes surrounding her home and photographed the family she loved. The family photographs are both formal and candid images. In observing her tenacity and devotion to taking pictures, another uncle, employed as a chemistry professor at nearby Rutgers University, taught her how to transpose the glass plates of the images she

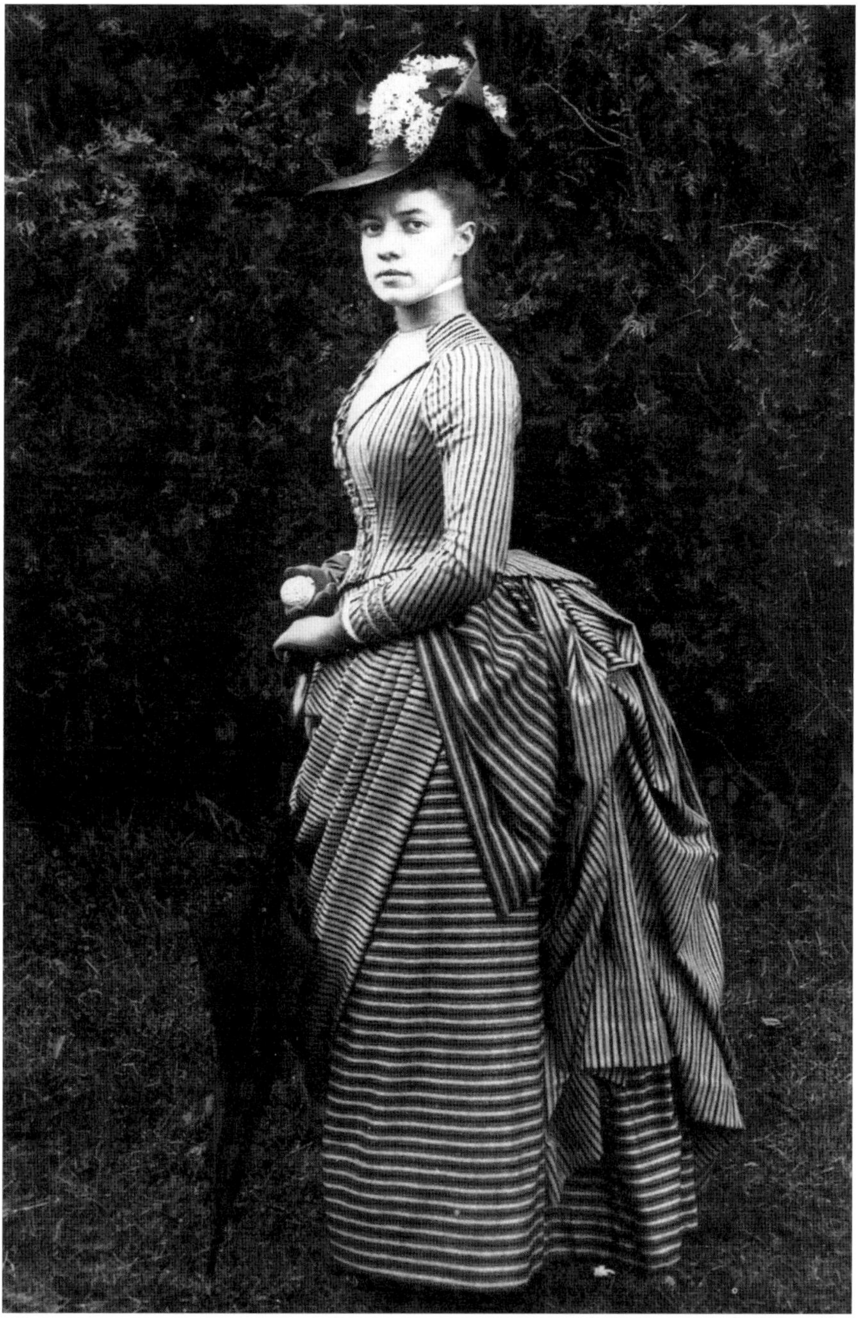

A portrait of Alice Austen at the age of twenty-two. *New York Public Library Digital Collection.*

took and make prints from them. Seeing how talented she was with the camera, her uncles built her a tiny darkroom where she would tirelessly spend hours developing the glass plates. Once she mastered the processing of photographs, Alice's love for the camera deepened. She became skilled at adjusting the lens, using the large equipment and traveling everywhere on Staten Island with her camera in tow.

At the Alice Austen Museum, descriptions of her life and her journeys are well documented. It is there her story is told beautifully and illustriously in the form of pictures. As she grew older and well into her teens, the vibrant woman added self-portraits to her photography portfolio. Also an avid athlete, Alice participated in many new sports brought to the Island, taking up tennis and cycling. She actively photographed the sports she loved, as well as their athletes and spectators. Alice had a deep, devoted passion for horticulture as well. She tended to the vast and beautiful gardens on the grounds of the family's one-acre home. Some of her most poignant and emotionally moving pieces are her photographs of the immigrants of New York City. Her countless images captured their vulnerability and uncertainty in a new world. Her talent and her camera lens garnered mesmerizing pictures depicting the life and times of the people of the nineteenth century.

Resulting from her family's wealth, Alice was afforded the opportunity to travel beyond the boundaries of Staten Island and live quite comfortably. She visited upstate New York, Vermont and eventually Europe. In 1899, on one of her summer expeditions, she met and befriended Gertrude Tate. Gertrude had lived in Brooklyn with her own family and visited Alice quite often over the course of several years. The pair spent a lot of time together and often enjoyed summer holidays overseas. However, their relationship was much to the dismay of Gertrude's family, and they strongly objected to their association. Gertrude eventually left Brooklyn, moved into Clear Comfort and became Alice's lifelong companion.

Alice lived off the interest from the money she inherited from her grandfather, enabling her to become a prominent figure in society and live a privileged life. According to aliceausten.org, she was a member of the Richmond County Country Club, located on Todt Hill in Staten Island, and also a member of the Colony Club in Manhattan. She also founded the Staten Island Garden Club in 1914.

However, the stock market crash of 1929 and the Great Depression changed Alice's life dramatically. Losing all her principal money in the Wall Street crash, her wealth diminished rapidly. Out of desperation and so she wouldn't lose her home, Clear Comfort, to the bank, she sold its artwork, furniture and some of her family's belongings to pay for its expenses. Upon dissolving the last of her personal items, she asked her friend Loring McMillen from the Staten Island Historical Society to hold onto her precious collection of glass plate negatives that contained the images of all her photographs. In 1945, Alice found her financial attempts had failed, and the bank repossessed Clear Comfort. Gertrude and Alice attempted living together in a small apartment for a period of time, but unfortunately, they couldn't afford to pay the rent. With such financial hardship thrust upon them, Gertrude moved back in with her family, and it was made clear Alice wasn't welcome. On June 24, 1950, Alice declared herself a pauper and joined the Staten Island Farm Colony, a home for the local poor, as told in Amy Khoudari's *Looking in the Shadows: The Life of Alice Austen*.

Clear Comfort, named by Alice's grandmother, was in the Austen family for one hundred years, and in the beginning, it was a humble eighteenth-century Dutch farmhouse. Over the course of time, as the family became more financially endowed, extensive renovations were made to the home. Alice's grandfather renovated the residence and transformed it into a magnificent Victorian cottage. He added rooms, extravagant windows and a picturesque covered porch to complement its beauty and style. Her grandfather, an avid gardener and lover of horticulture, designed the exterior grounds of the home with wrapping Japanese wisteria vines, blossoming trees and colorful floral gardens. Upon the demise of Alice's wealth, this lavish and quaint home fell into disrepair, and years of neglect soon followed.

With the travesty of living in a poorhouse thrust upon Alice, the most ironic twist of fate occurred. In 1950, the publishing company Picture Press began a project on historical American women and contacted the Staten Island Historical Society for recommendations. It was then that friends McMillen and C. Copes Brinley shared Alice's glass plate negatives of eight thousand unpublished images with the publisher. A select handful were chosen and published in Oliver Jensen's book *Revolt of Women*. He also published a story about Alice in *Life* magazine and published some of her travel photos in *Holiday* magazine. The monies generated from the published photographs were enough to move her from the poorhouse and into a private nursing facility. On October 9, 1951, Alice was the guest of honor at the first Alice Austen Day, where she saw an exhibition of her work. Her response to the events of that day was quoted in the *New York Times* article "Old Friends Honor Miss Alice Austen. Photographer for 50 Years Has Her Day": "I am happy that what was once so much pleasure for me turns out now to be a pleasure for other people."

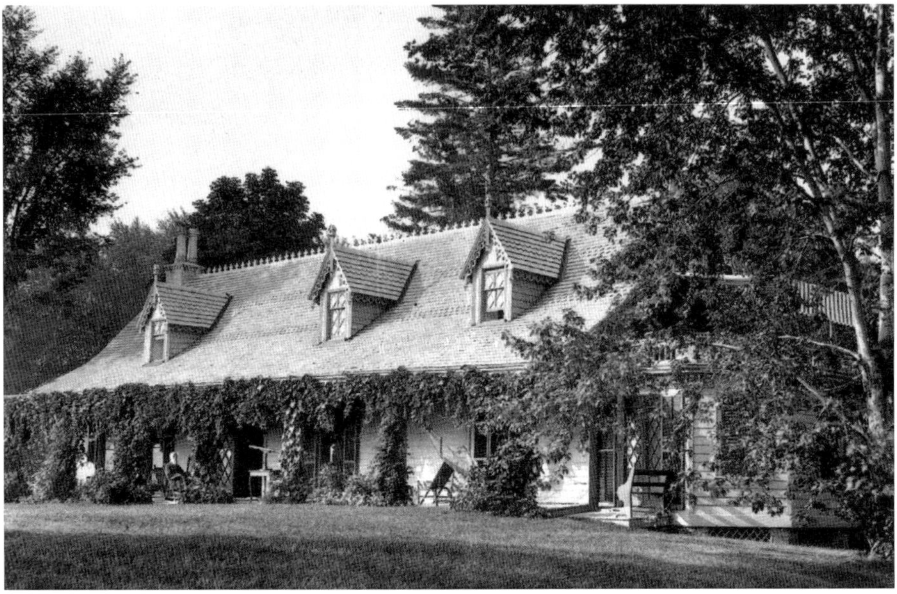

The home of Alice Austen, which is named Clear Comfort. *New York Public Library Digital Collection.*

Alice Austen passed away on June 9, 1952. She is buried in the Austen family plot in Moravian Cemetery, Staten Island. Gertrude and Alice's final wishes were to be buried together, but it was denied by their families.

As documented on aliceausten.org, during the 1960s several supporters took matters into their own hands to save Clear Comfort and its grounds. The Alice Austen House was included in the National Register of Historic Places in 1970, and money was granted from New York City's capital budget for restoration to begin. Clear Comfort became a New York City Landmark in 1971 and a National Historic Landmark in 1993. The Staten Island Historical Society continues to support the Alice Austen House, and the collection is stored in Historic Richmond Town. Alice Austen has a Staten Island school and a Staten Island ferry named in her honor.

Today, the Alice Austen House Museum is restored to its original splendor, adorned with beautiful gardens. It is open to the public for tours, offering an expansive exhibit of Alice Austen's photographs. The exhibit is a testament to one of Staten Island's most gifted photographers, a woman who defined her life by creativity and perseverance.

THE GARIBALDI-MEUCCI MUSEUM

The Garibaldi-Meucci Museum was once the home of Italian inventor Antonio Meucci and his wife. Having moved to America in 1850, they came to the United States with their savings and settled in Staten Island, where they would reside for the rest of their lives. The inventor used some of the rooms in his home as laboratories for his many inventions and research and also designated an area in the home for his candle-making factory. As mentioned in Sandra Meucci's book *Antonio and the Electric Scream: The Man Who Invented the Telephone*, it is said the Meucci family welcomed into their home fellow Italian friends who were escaping political prosecution during Italy's turbulent years fighting for unification. Seeking refuge, their guests would live with them and also gain employment in Meucci's factory. One such inhabitant was fellow Italian and friend Giuseppe Garibaldi, the well-known Italian revolutionary. He lived with Antonio and his wife for several years, commanding merchant ships in and out of New York Harbor, and also found employment in Meucci's candle-making factory, as documented in "History of the House" at garibaldimeuccimuseum.org.

A plaque was placed on Antonio Meucci's residence in 1854 in honor of the Italian revolutionary, commemorating his time living in the humble 1840s cottage on Staten Island. The home, formerly known as the Garibaldi Memorial, was celebrated as Garibaldi's temporary residence, as mentioned in the 1907 article "Italians Dedicate Garibaldi Memorial" in the *New York Times*. Subsequently, the original clapboard farmhouse was relocated and placed within a columned pavilion. The dedication of its new site coincided with Garibaldi's 100th birthday, as mentioned in the 1917 *New York Times* article "Italian Commission to Honor Garibaldi." In 1923, a memorial in Antonio Meucci's honor was placed at the front entryway.

As mentioned in William J. Wallace's ruling, "Globe Telephone Company, 1884—Famous ATT Patent Fight: 1996–2007," it is noted that Meucci's primary source of income from 1859 to 1861 came from benefactors solely interested in his inventions and experiments.

Financial strife, bankruptcy and poverty struck Meucci as a direct result of fraudulent debtors and the closing of his candle factory. His home was auctioned off in 1861, but the purchaser allowed him and his wife to live there rent free. His wife, an invalid, died a few years later. Toward the later part of his life, Meucci had very little money and became dependent on public assistance for financial support. He fell ill in 1889 and died later the same year.

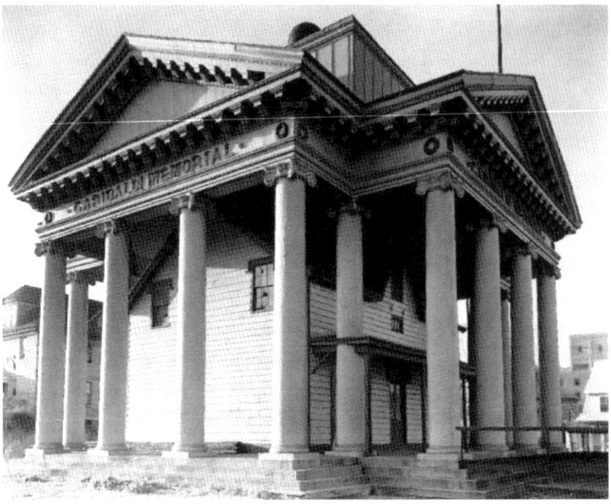

Left: The Garibaldi Memorial,1932. *New York Public Library Collection.*

Below: The Garibaldi-Meucci Museum today. *Wikimedia Commons.*

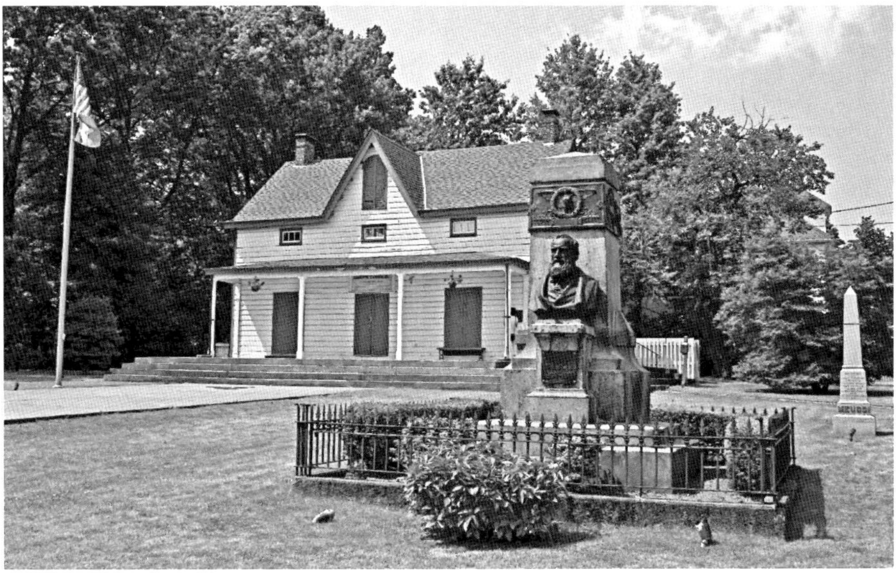

Today, the site of the Meucci home is known as the Garibaldi-Meucci Museum and is restored to the glory of its early days. Furthermore, it no longer remains within the structured columns. Opened in 1956, it is owned by the National Order Sons of Italy Foundation and run by the New York Grand Lodge Order Sons of Italy in America. It is located in the Rosebank neighborhood of Staten Island.

The Garibaldi-Meucci Museum was added to the U.S. National Register of Historic Places in 1980 and contains artifacts from Antonio Meucci's inventions, including his model renderings, photographs, personal drawings and personal memorabilia. The giant cauldron he used in his candle-making factory is also on display. Giuseppe Garibaldi's military uniforms and rifles are also on exhibit, along with several collections of his medals. The museum honors these outstanding Italian men and their achievements and contributions to society. The museum pays tribute to the long-standing values of Italian culture and Italian-American heritage. It offers the public classes in Italian language, guided tours, museum exhibits and lectures in Italian culture, from "Life in Ancient Rome" to "Carnevale in Venice."

Antonio Meucci

Antonio Meucci is the remarkable Italian inventor most known for inventing a prototype of the telephone. The controversy over whether he or Alexander Graham Bell is more deserving of its credit as inventor has been a much-debated topic for years. Although the United States credits Bell and he is the recipient of its patent, the Italian government credits Meucci with its invention.

The inventor and his wife immigrated to New York in the mid-1800s. Arriving with all their savings in hand, they moved to Staten Island, where they lived in a small cottage. Antonio Meucci operated his candle-making factory there, conducted an array of experiments and developed many inventions. One specific invention was the development of a voice-communication model, which many credit as the first telephone.

Meucci dedicated some of the rooms in his home for his candle-making factory and had a laboratory in his basement for his experiments. Much of his savings were spent on patents and their expensive application fees for his many inventions, and as a result, much of his money dwindled through the course of the years.

In 1856, Meucci began experimenting with electromagnetic transmissions using voice through the wires. These principles were based on his scientific experiments conducted within the confines of his home, as mentioned in Sandra Meucci's *Antonio and the Electric Scream*. The book states that Meucci designed a device that allowed his voice to transmit from his laboratory in the basement to his bedridden wife on the second floor of the home. Some of his notes, from "History of the House," describe his principal thoughts: "It consists of a vibrating diaphragm and an electrified magnet with a spiral wire that wraps around it. The vibrating diaphragm alters the current of the magnet. These alterations of current, transmitted

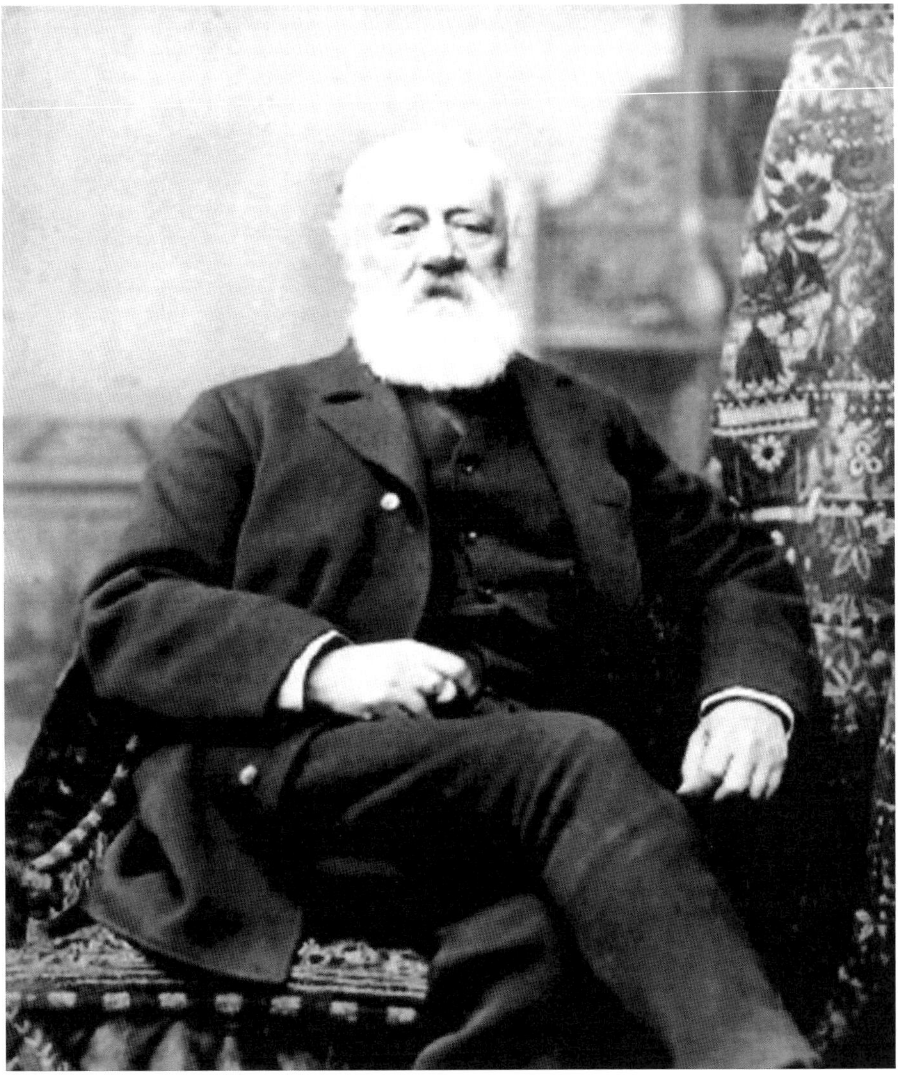

Portrait of Italian inventor Antonio Meucci. *Wikimedia Commons.*

to the other end of the wire, create analogous vibrations of the receiving diaphragm and reproduce the word."

Based on these principles, he continued to develop and experiment with over twenty types of models. In the late 1800s, artist and fellow Italian Nestore Corradi drew sketches of his designs, according to the Italian Society of Electrotechnics. The sketches were reproduced as a stamp and used by the Italian Postal and Telegraph Society. Meucci was financially supported by investors interested in his experiments between 1859 through 1861.

In 1871, Meucci had an agreement with the secretary of the Italian consulate in New York and several business associates to establish the Telettrofono Company and paid fifteen dollars to file an application for a patent. Although his attorney submitted a caveat titled "Sound Telegraph" to the U.S. Patent Office in 1871, there is no mention of electromagnetic transmission of vocal sound in it. Shortly thereafter, Meucci's wife died, and financial turmoil fell upon him: he lost funding for his experiments, his candle-making business went bankrupt and he lost his home. He never financially recovered and couldn't afford to renew his sound telegraph caveat. Sandra Meucci's *Antonio and the Electric Scream* mentions that some sixteen years later, "Alexander Graham Bell was given a patent for the electromagnetic transmission of vocal sound by undulating electric current."

There has been much controversy over who deserves the recognition as the inventor of the telephone, although Bell is credited with its discovery by the United States. The Federazione Italiana di Elettrotecnica credits Meucci as the real inventor, and the Italian government honors him as the "official inventor of the telephone." Bell's patents were defended in hundreds of cases. In 2002, Representative Vito Fossella (R-NY) presented to the U.S. House of Representatives House Resolution 269, referencing Antonio Meucci: "The life and achievements of Antonio Meucci should be recognized, and his work in the invention of the telephone should be acknowledged."

The resolution also claims, "If Meucci had been able to pay the $10 fee to maintain the caveat after 1874, no patent could have been issued to Bell."

Giuseppe Garibaldi

Noted as one of Italy's most resounding revolutionaries, Giuseppe Garibaldi was a decorated Italian general and nationalist. Garibaldi was a merchant navy captain and heavily involved in coastal trades all over the globe.

In 1833, on an excursion to Russia, he met Giovanni Battista, a member of a secret society known as the Young Italy Movement of Giuseppe Mazzini. Its passionate mission was to unify Italy as a republic and free it from Austrian dominance. Garibaldi joined forces with this operation, but it wasn't too long before political persecution threatened him in Piedmont. According to "Giuseppe Garibaldi (Italian Revolutionary)" at www.britannica.com/biography/Giuseppe-Garibaldi, he fled to Brazil and eventually joined the

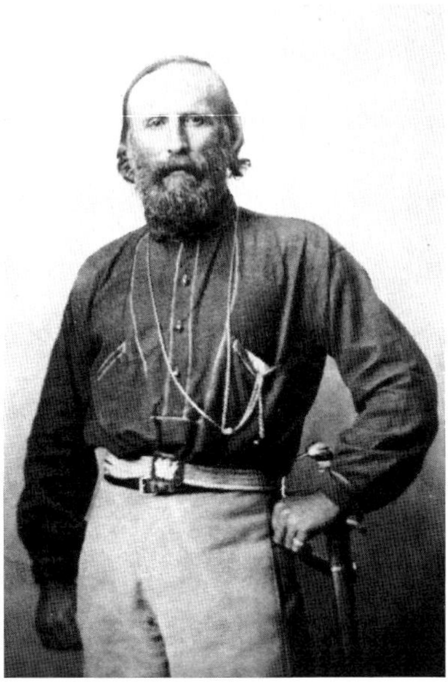

Portrait of Italian revolutionary Giuseppe Garibaldi. *Library of Congress.*

Republic of Rio Grande do Sul. He aided its causes in separating from the Brazilian Empire and joined the rebels known as Ragamuffins in the Ragamuffin War. By 1841, Garibaldi had relocated to Uruguay, worked as a trader and schoolmaster and was married with children. It was during this phase of his life that he adopted his trademark clothing of gauchos, ponchos, red shirts and sombreros. Continuing his passions for liberation, Garibaldi became involved in the Uruguayan civil war. He was commander of the Uruguayan fleet, with an "Italian legion" of soldiers referred to as "Red Shirts." The moniker came about because of their bloused red shirt uniforms, which became the symbol of all his volunteers.

Yearning for his homeland and with growing concerns about the Italian states and their battles, Garibaldi returned to Italy. He stayed there for several years, commanding soldiers in the Republican army. He led his legions to many victories, including one against the French army. However, at the Siege of Rome, after more French reinforcements were sent in, Garibaldi and his army were defeated. He commanded his troops to retreat to the north, but many fled because they were hunted by the French, Spanish and Austrians, as cited in G.M. Trevelyan's *Garibaldi's Defense of the Roman Republic*. Garibaldi got as far north as Porto Venere, but during the retreat from Rome, his wife died. Once in the north, the government of Piedmont forced his exile once again, and this time he came to America with the intentions of commanding a merchant ship that was financed by businessmen. Upon his arrival in 1850, much to his dismay, Garibaldi found the funding for the ship never came to fruition. He mingled with fellow revolutionaries and resided with Italian inventor Antonio Meucci and his wife on Staten Island for several years. Garibaldi financially sustained himself while living in America as an employee in Meucci's candle-making factory and, according to his autobiography, *The Autobiography of Giuseppe Garibaldi*, also made a living as a commander of merchant ships that sailed in and out of New York Harbor. His autobiography documents many of his voyages across the Pacific Ocean.

In 1854, Garibaldi returned to Italy in an area north of Sardinia, but not long after his return, war broke out in the Sardinian region. Committed to his country and its people, he entered battle once again. The wars extended into Sicily, where he commanded armies and ultimately became known as the dictator of Sicily, as noted in *A History of the Western World*, written by Shepard B. Clough. Until his death in 1860, Giuseppe Garibaldi remained valiant and courageous. Always found in the center of militia campaigns commanding countless armies and impassioned by a love for his country, the revolutionary general is celebrated as one of the founding fathers of Italy's unification.

HISTORIC RICHMOND TOWN

An area in Staten Island where time stands still is called Historic Richmond Town. This quaint village spans over twenty-five acres and is home to more than thirty historic buildings between one hundred and three hundred years old, farms and museums. It is American history at its finest, located conveniently in the center of Staten Island.

The original settlement of this area occurred in the late 1600s, when the town was known as Cocclestown, a reference to the large quantity of oyster shells in the vicinity. Much later, in the 1800s, the area became a hub of commercial activity for the community, where the courthouse of Richmond County was a focal point, as noted in *The Encyclopedia of New York*.

The nineteenth-century residents of this historic town were mostly of Dutch, English or French heritage, and during the American Revolution, British troops were stationed here. In the village, craftsman shops such as blacksmiths, shoemakers, candle makers, basket makers, carpenter shops and markets were part of the daily life and function of this town. Furthermore, adjacent to Richmond Town are St. Andrew's Episcopal Church, St. Patrick's Roman Catholic Church and Mount Richmond Cemetery, which is operated by the Hebrew Free Burial Association.

As noted on historicrichmondtown.org, the preservation of Historic Richmond Town today is due to the commitment of many Staten Islanders, especially dedicated Staten Island historians William T. Davis and Loring McMillen and banker David L. Decker. In 1958, Historic Richmond Town was established as a result of the partnership between the Staten Island Historical Society (a nonprofit cultural organization) and the City of New York. The city owns the historical buildings and the land, and a portion of its operations are funded by the Department of Cultural Affairs.

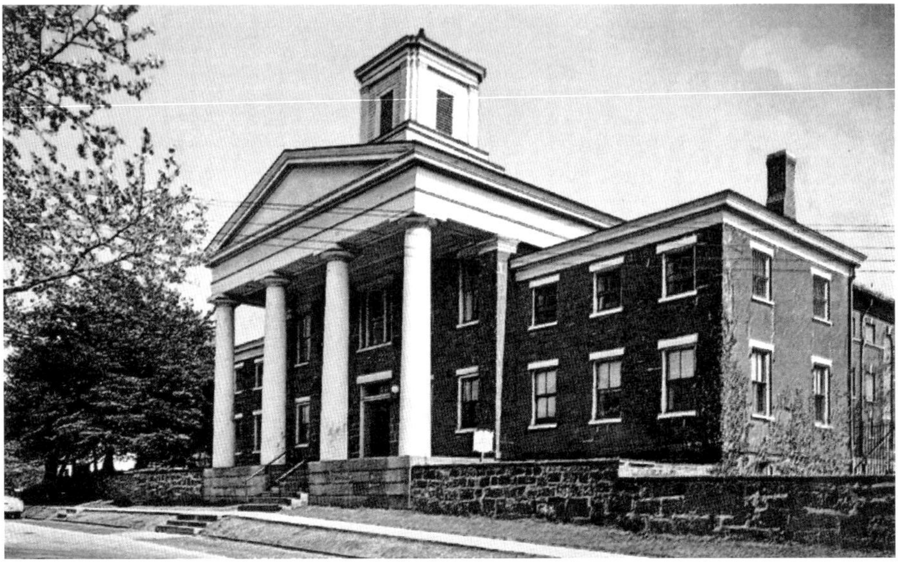

Above: Richmond Town Courthouse, in historic Richmond Town. *New York Public Library Collection.*

Right: St. Andrew's Church, built in 1709, and a view of its cemetery. It is one of the oldest churches on Staten Island. *New York Public Library Collection.*

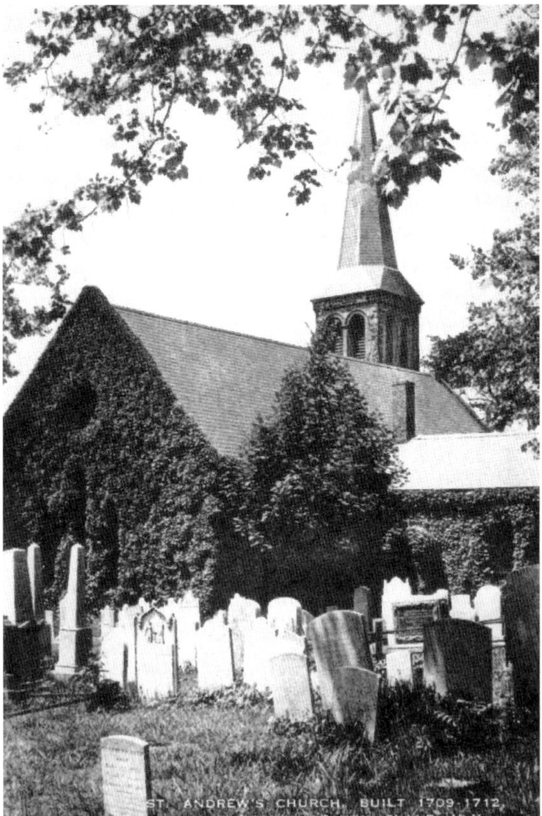

Today, visitors have the unique opportunity to visit Historic Richmond Town and experience firsthand what it was like to have lived during the colonial era. To walk along graveled paths lined by one-hundred-year-old oak trees and appreciate the timeless beauty of a once-vibrant town is a treat for everyone of all ages. One can only imagine how life used to be so many decades ago. From seeing the Voorlezer's House, the oldest exhibit in the village (which, incidentally, is the oldest elementary school in the United States, dating back to 1695), to the 1740 Dutch Colonial farmhouse called the Guyon-Lake-Tysen House, these historical landmarks are wonders to the eye. Furthermore, structural examples of Dutch Colonial and Greek Revival architecture are found in the Stephens-Black House and Decker Farm.

Historic Richmond Town offers the public an opportunity to experience this delightful village, hosting special events such as the Richmond County Fair, seasonal festivals, pumpkin picking, guided tours, candlelight tours, Old Home Day, English Country Dancing and quilt classes, to name just a few.

Historic Richmond Town takes great pride in the research, preservation and restoration of the historical grounds and artifacts that define Staten Island's early history.

The Kreischer Mansion

In the mid-1800s, a German immigrant by the name of Balthasar Kreischer established his fire brick manufacturing business on the western shore of Staten Island. As noted in Robert Sietsema's 2010 article "Killmeyer's and the Kreischer Mansion: Meat and Murder in Staten Island" in the *Village Voice*, the area is where large amounts of clay deposit exist in the earth and proved beneficial as the ideal site for the factory and the fabrication of fire bricks. The factory yielded a fortune for Balthasar Kreischer and his family. Today, Clay Pit Pond State Preserve is located not far from where the factory once stood and where the Kreischer Mansion currently is situated. According to *Atlas Obscura*, the company's success brought such grand economic wealth to the area that it became known as Kreischerville. Today, this section of Staten Island is referred to as the beautiful neighborhood of Charleston.

To further expand his wealth in the town, the brick magnate purchased several acres of land atop what was called Kreischer Hill. In 1885, the wealthy Kreischer built identical massive mansions for his sons, Charles and Edward. The grand homes were beautifully designed in Victorian-style architecture. The mansions, two-story structures, had verandas, decorative

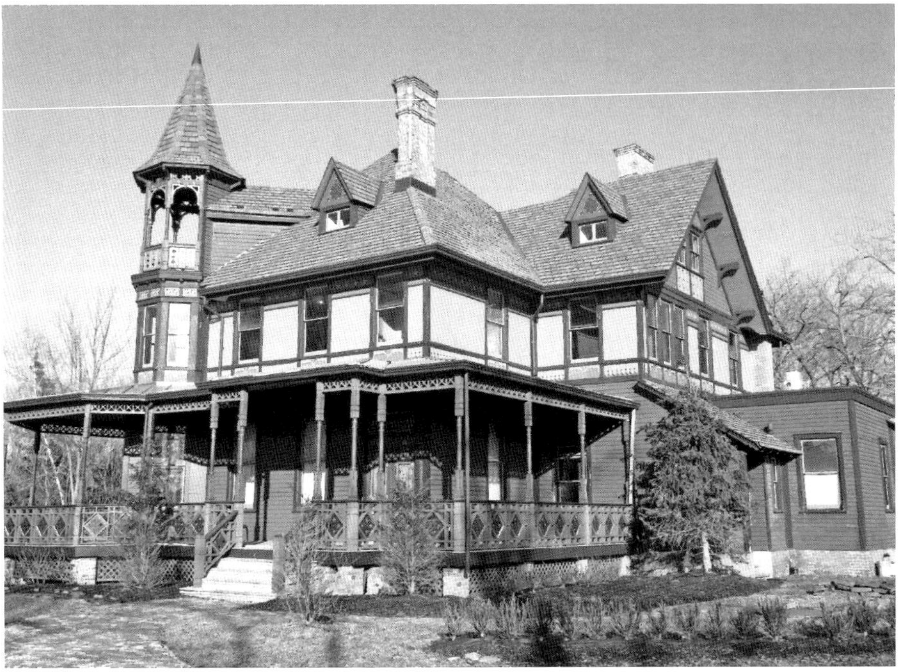

The Kreischer Mansion. *Wikimedia Commons.*

railings, corner towers and gables and decorative grounds. As described in Steve Lehto's *American Murder Houses: A Coast-to-Coast Tour of the Most Notorious Houses of Homicide*, the interior of the homes had a multitude of sumptuous rooms as living spaces, almost every room had carved fireplaces and there were twelve-foot ceilings, opulent chandeliers and decorative leather wallpaper.

Tragically, in 1886, one year after the elaborate residences were completed, Balthasar died, and an ironic series of events ensued. The brick manufacturing company that had financially sustained the family with such wealth fell victim to a fire and burned to the ground. Through hardships and disappointment, the family never fully recovered from the devastating loss and were unable to regain economic stability. In 1894, Edward Kreischer committed suicide by gruesomely shooting himself in the head in his home, and brother Charles's home was destroyed during the Great Depression, as documented in *Atlas Obscura*.

For many years, Edward's mansion, the sole remaining one left on the mass of land at the top of the hill, became the subject of ghost tales.

Strange sightings, eerie noises and flickering lights became associated with the home, as documented in Hilke Schellmann's 2012 *Wall Street Journal* article "Spirits Moving on S.I." Also mentioned in Robert Sietsema's 2010 *Village Voice* article "Killmeyer's and the Kreischer Mansion: Meat and Murder in Staten Island," many locals speak of the home's legendary spooky tales; in one, it is believed the spirit of Edward's wife is crying and wailing through the house, mourning the death of her beloved. Another myth suggests the murdered German cook haunts the halls, banging pots and pans. Nonetheless, the home remains a favorite spot for children on Halloween.

The home changed hands multiple times over the course of decades and was added to the National Register of Historic Places in 1982, according to the National Park Service. A short-lived Victorian restaurant attempted to succeed there but failed in 1997. Shortly thereafter, as mentioned in Diane C. Lore's 2016 article "Staten Island's Kreischer Mansion Up for Sale for $9.5 Million" in the *Staten Island Advance*, a prominent real estate developer purchased the five-acre estate for $1.4 million in 1999. His dream was to build a luxury community, naming it Kreischerville, in honor of Kreischer himself. The developer restored the mansion, but the grander projects were put on hold due to the instability in the real estate market, financial strain and delays.

In 2005, the Kreischer Mansion was home to a murder. Joseph "Joe Black" Young, caretaker of the mansion, used the house as the site to commit a vicious, grisly murder. According to the *New York Times* article "Grisly Mob Killing at S.I. Mansion Is Detailed," written in 2016 by William K. Rashbaum, the caretaker of the property stabbed, drowned and then dismembered the body of Robert McKelvey. He then disposed of the body by burning it in the home's furnace. In 2008, it became known that the culprit was affiliated with the Bonanno crime family, and the murdered victim was a rival mob associate.

The Kreischer Mansion still stands today in all its splendor and beauty on the hilltop, offering treetop views of Staten Island and New Jersey. The home has been used for fashion shoots, movie locations and, as mentioned in Lehto's *American Murder Houses*, most recently appeared in HBO's *Boardwalk Empire*. Today, the Kreischer Mansion is privately owned and no longer open to the public.

MOUNT LORETTO

Mount Loretto was founded by Father John Christopher Drumgoole, an Irish Roman Catholic priest in the late nineteenth century, and at one time was the largest orphanage in New York State.

Father John Christopher Drumgoole, born in 1816, came to America at nine years old. After the death of his father, he lived with his mother and worked as a shoemaker to help support her. He became a United States citizen in 1838.

By 1844, Father Drumgoole had found employment in Manhattan's St. Mary's Roman Catholic Church, and by that time, New York City had become overrun with homeless children who lived on its streets. Many children had lost their parents due to sickness from the long voyage to America or shortly after their arrival. Many children were also homeless as a result of the American Civil War in the United States and the Great Potato Famine in Ireland, as documented by Mallick Fitzpatrick in "John C. Drumgoole" from the *Catholic Encyclopedia*, vol. 5. These unfortunate children, often referred to as "street urchins," became victims of disease, malnutrition and poverty. Many of them tried to earn money as newsboys during the golden age of the American press. However, the publishers of major newspapers, handouts and weeklies exploited them. Although a law

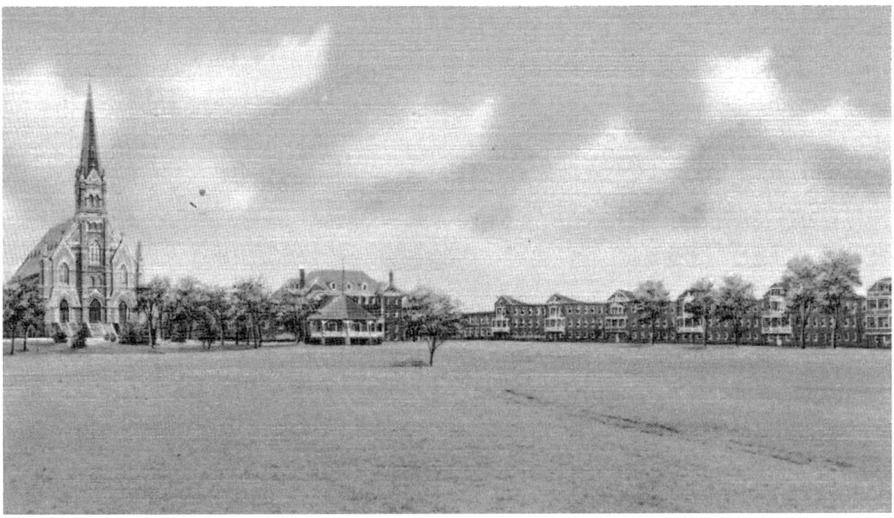

A postcard of the Mount Loretto buildings and grounds, circa early 1900s. The orphanage was founded by Father John C. Drumgoole in 1883. *New York Public Library Digital Collection.*

was passed in 1876 for their protection and banned their mistreatment, thousands upon thousands of children remained in the streets of New York City poverty stricken, notes author Peter J. Eckel in his article "Father Christopher C. Drumgoole, Shepherd of the Homeless Newsboys" for historyreference.org.

Father Drumgoole's humble beginnings in the land of opportunity instilled in him the desire to help others, especially the thousands of children who reflected his poverty-stricken youth. He grew concerned for their welfare and devoted himself to helping them through these difficult times as best he could. He began using the basement of St. Mary's Church, on the Lower East Side of Manhattan, to provide shelter to the many throngs of children who had no home.

Having entered priesthood late in life, Father Drumgoole was ordained at age fifty-nine in 1869, as documented in "Saints of New York: Father John C. Drumgoole" at nyfaithinformation.org. In 1871, Father Drumgoole began working for the St. Vincent de Paul Society in Manhattan. It is there he spearheaded the Newsboys' Lodging House. The response was overwhelming, and the house quickly became filled to capacity. Father Drumgoole decided the shelter was no longer adequate for the newsboys, and in a desire to seek funding to build a larger residence, he founded St. Joseph's Union and offered annual twenty-five-cent subscriptions to receive its newspaper, entitled *Homeless Child*. After several years of success with the mailer, he accrued enough funding to build a larger facility for the homeless children of New York City. According to "A Brief History of MIV" at mountloretto.org, a ten-story building was erected in 1881 on the corner of Great Jones and Lafayette Streets in Manhattan. It was called the Mission of the Immaculate Virgin and became the site of a new shelter. Although the new building was designed to allow in ample light and air for its residents, Father Drumgoole believed the general environment of a harsh, threatening city was not ideal or healthy for a child, but perhaps a more rural setting would be.

In 1882, he set out to Staten Island's South Shore and purchased a farm and several adjacent plots of land. It was named Mount Loretto, in honor of the nuns who taught and worked there with him. It was his goal to have the children reside on a self-sufficient farm and be exposed to vocational training.

Mount Loretto was gigantic in every conceivable way; the area encompassed almost two hundred acres. According to Eckel's article, the grand farm became one of the most productive ones on Staten Island,

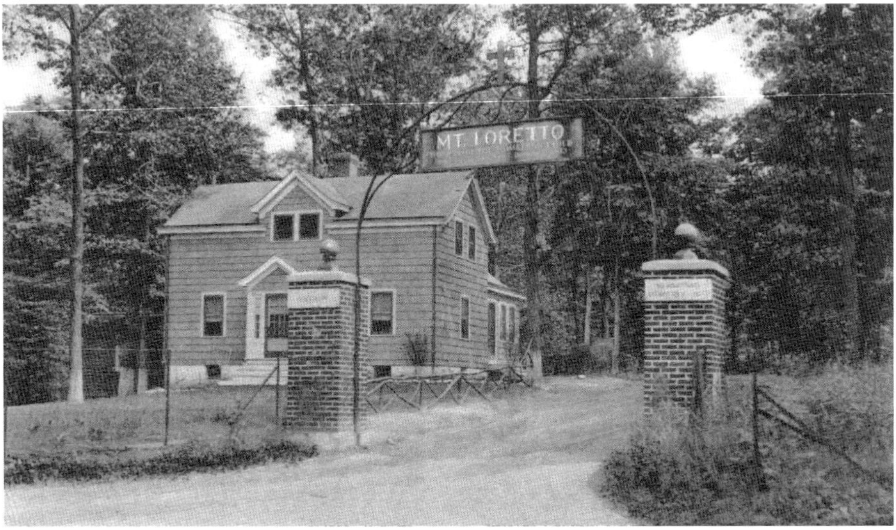

The entranceway to Mount Loretto, circa late 1800s. *New York Public Library Collection.*

where fields were plowed and cultivated, and it produced all the food for the mission. In addition to the buildings on the property, there was a large henhouse and a massive barn that stood over five stories high that housed over three hundred heads of cattle and horses. The property, full of freshwater wetlands and bluffs facing the ocean, was home to native plants and abundant wildlife. Additionally, the historic stone lighthouse, Prince's Bay Light, which is a New York State Landmark today, was perched on the land's highest bluff. One of the most breathtaking sites on the Mount Loretto grounds was its magnificent church, completed in 1894; its steeple rose 225 feet in the air.

As the orphans thrived in their new environment, Father Drumgoole persevered in his quest to continue to enrich their lives. He and the sisters provided them with the essentials of learning vocational trades. Being taught the skills of cooking, farming, woodworking, printing and shoemaking ensured that one day the newsboys could financially sustain themselves as adults. In fact, most of the pews, wood trim and doors in the Mount Loretto church were made by the orphans. The mission, committed to providing homeless "street urchins" a healthy, safe, educational environment, housed and cared for almost two thousand boys and girls at one point.

Father Drumgoole was committed to both of his organizations and split his time between Mount Loretto in Staten Island and the Mission of the

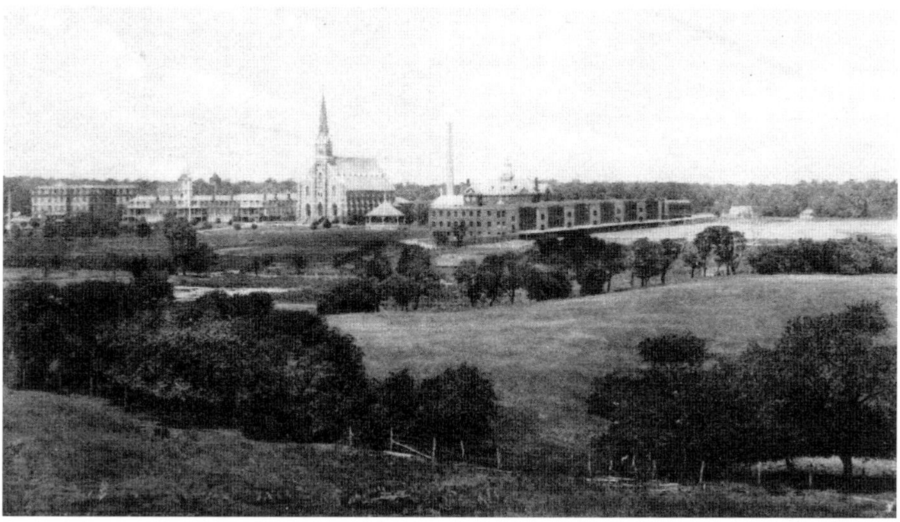

A view of the Mount Loretto orphanage from a nearby hill. *New York Public Library Collection.*

Immaculate Virgin in Manhattan. In March, he was caught in the Great Blizzard of 1888. While attempting to get back to the mission in Manhattan, Father Drumgoole arrived at Staten Island's Ferry Terminal, but because of gusty winds and poor visibility due to the terrible storm conditions, all ferries were canceled. In an attempt to get back to Mount Loretto, he hired a horse and carriage on the South Shore of the Island. After that terrible storm, he fell ill and tragically died several weeks later at the age of seventy-two from pneumonia. Father Drumgoole was debt free and bequeathed all his belongings to the mission.

In 1894, a memorial statue was erected in his honor at the Manhattan mission site, as documented in the 1894 *New York Times* article "Father Drumgoole Honored." The statue was transferred to Mount Loretto in 1920. The statue is of Father Drumgoole standing with two young boys; one boy is well dressed and reading a book, and the other is a ragged newsboy clinging to the priest. The statue is meant to symbolize the same child, depicting the newsboys before and after their time at the mission. Over the years, many of Mount Loretto's buildings have been destroyed. In the 1970s, the church was used in the movie *The Godfather*; however, shortly after filming, the church was destroyed in a fire. Today, only its magnificent façade remains.

This selfless man, his compelling life story and his dedication to the betterment of children is remarkable. Father Drumgoole's passion to create

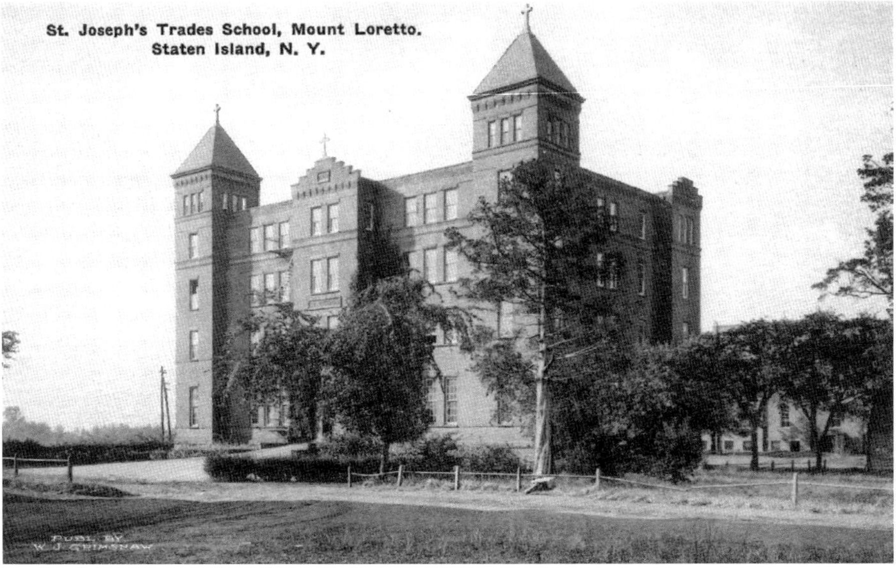

St. Joseph's Trades School, the vocational school for the orphans residing at Mount Loretto. *New York Public Library Digital Collection.*

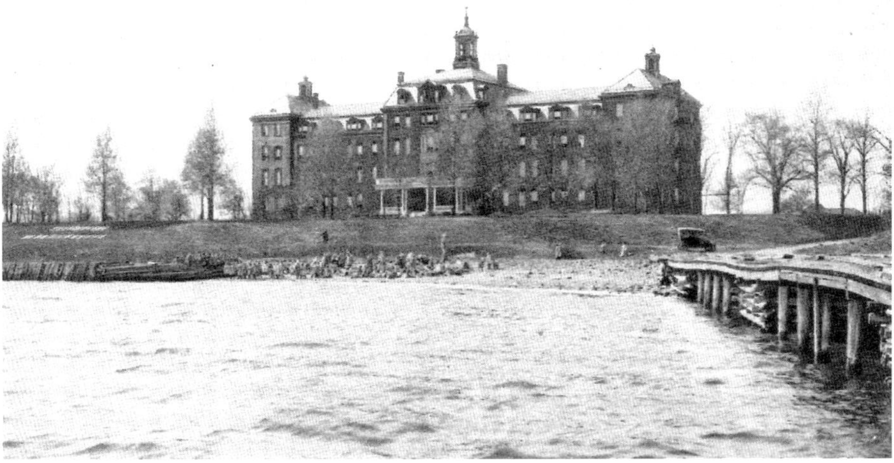

The girls' dormitory and home on the Mount Loretto property. *New York Public Library Collection.*

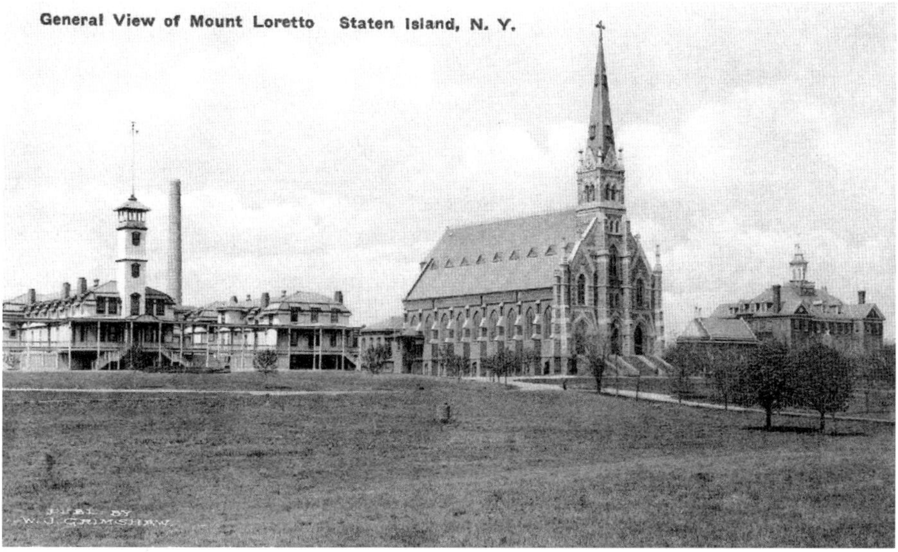

General view of the buildings and magnificent church on the Mount Loretto grounds. *New York Public Library Collection.*

a better world for so many unfortunate is inspirational. In tribute to him, a Staten Island boulevard and an elementary school bear his name.

Although Mount Loretto ended all foster care contracts with New York City in 1995 and the land was purchased by the New York State Department of Environmental Conservation in 1999, it continues to foster partnerships with several social service agencies on Staten Island. Operating as a nonprofit agency of the Archdiocese of New York, Mount Loretto remains passionate and committed to the services it offers the community. On the palatial grounds are a daycare, a senior center, a vocational training program, an individualized care facility for challenged individuals and a community youth center.

THE SEGUINE-BURKE MANSION

In 1786, a gentleman named James Seguine purchased a very large parcel of land located on Lemon Creek near the South Shore of Staten Island with sweeping views of Prince's Bay.

According to Historic Houses Trust at historichousetrust.org, the house remained in the Seguine family and was passed down to James's great-grandson Joseph Seguine. Joseph maintained the family oyster business and helped develop the Staten Island Railroad Company. He also founded the Staten Island Oil and Candle Making Company. The family had acquired a tidy fortune from its oyster farming business on the island, and with his added entrepreneurial investments, Joseph added to its considerable wealth. Joseph went on to purchase more land in the adjacent areas and, in 1836, built a grand mansion on his property in Staten Island.

The estate reflected the family's wealth in the most definitive of ways. The two-story home with six grandiose columns faced the ocean, offering breathtaking views. Its interior was ornate and elaborate, indicative of the lifestyles of prominent businessmen of that era. The home had Greek Revival mantels and spacious rooms with elongated windows and doors to allow the free-flowing breezes of the ocean to travel through the home. In front of the home was the grand lawn. The property also housed a stable, a hay barn and a carriage house.

Joseph Seguine died in 1856, and right after the Civil War, the family fortune dwindled away, leaving the family to fall into financial despair. They

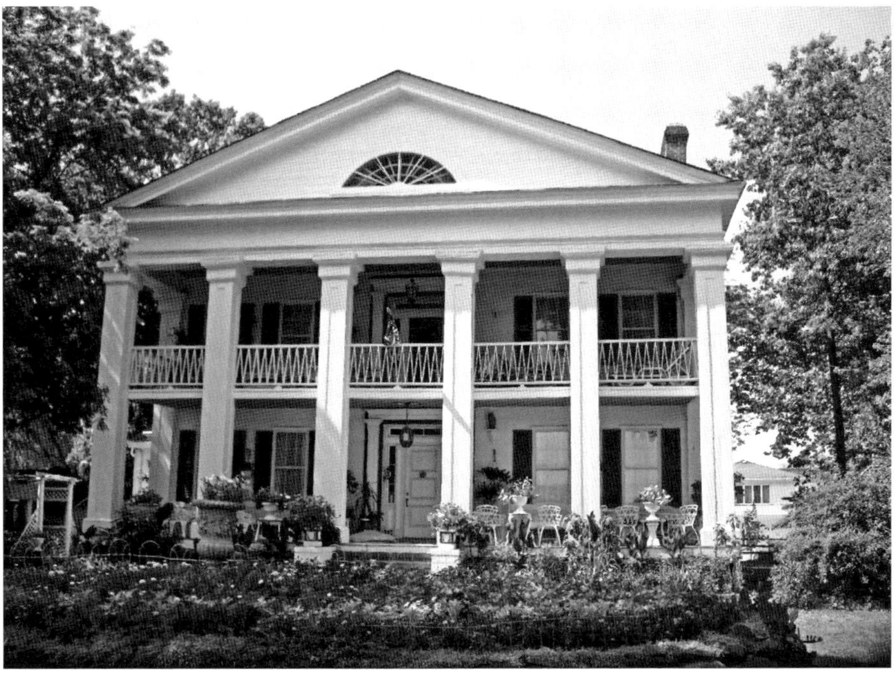

The Seguine-Burke Mansion. *Wikimedia Commons.*

sold their property and home in 1868. In 1916, Joseph's great-grandson purchased ten acres of the property back, along with the mansion. He lived there with his wife, Bess, and their two daughters until his death in 1981. According to Shayla Love's 2014 article "Inside Seguine Mansion, Staten Island's Eccentric Historic Home" at gothamist.com, Bess and Joseph's daughters relocated, and Bess moved to Georgia, leaving the home abandoned. It fell victim to vultures as it was robbed, vandalized and left in disrepair. Bess wanted to sell the Seguine home but only to a buyer who respected its history and beauty as much as she did. Shayla Love further mentions the current owner, George Burke, and his affiliation with the home.

Apparently, George Burke was a school friend of the Seguine daughters and frequented the Seguine home many times during its heyday. He always admired the home and made it a point to say so to Bess. Burke joined the U.S. Air Force at nineteen and lived in Europe. He didn't return to Staten Island for many years, but remembering his fondness for her home, Bess sought him out and convinced him to buy it. In Shayla Love's article, Burke is quoted as having made a journal entry that reads:

> *I made my way through the heavy under growth that had covered the front lawn. About two hundred feet in front of the mansion, I looked back. In spite of the decay that started to engulf the house, the mansion stood in its breathtaking splendor. I knew then, i was lost in what seemed a hopeless fight to save and restore this grand old mansion. So be it.*

George Burke purchased the Seguine mansion in 1981. The renovations took five years and all of Burke's money. Many of his family and friends donated their time to help him restore it back to its original beauty. Wanting to protect the home's illustrious history, he decided he wanted to donate the historic mansion. He approached the New York City Department of Parks and Recreation and negotiated a business deal. In 1989, he donated the Seguine House to the City of New York, and in exchange for all his financial investments in renovation, he was granted permission to continue to reside in the residence and retain an interest in the mansion for the remainder of his life.

This unique situation also split the care of the home. The parks department pays the taxes and the water bills and is expected to take care of everything on the outside of the mansion; Burke is responsible for maintaining everything inside the mansion. However, he still maintains the exterior anyway. He plants and tends to the massive flower beds of blooming daffodils and tulips and the grand lawn, where aquamarine- and teal-colored peacocks roam free. The stables on the grounds operate as an equestrian center and provide a small income to financially subsidize the property. Additionally, the Friends of Seguine Mansion, a not-for-profit organization, manages tours of the home and its annual fundraising events: a spring garden party, a fall period-costume barbecue and a black-tie Christmas formal to assist in the care and maintenance of the residence and its grounds. The elaborate home is decorated with all of Burke's antiques and artwork from his days abroad many years ago. Today, the mansion is known as the Seguine-Burke Mansion, and George Burke lives there with his dog tending to the property he loves.

THE WILLIAM T. AND MARY MARCELLITE GARNER MANSION

The William T. and Mary Marcellite Garner mansion is monumental in size, depicting the Second Empire style of design. This massive two-story brownstone structure features a four-story tower on its west side. It has Tuscan columns that open onto a recessed porch, and the multiple levels of its roof still retain their arched dormers.

The home was originally purchased in 1870 by William T. Garner, an extremely wealthy businessman. He was the owner of one of the country's largest textile mills, Harmony Mills. He was also the vice commodore of the New York Yacht Club. At the time, Garner is said to have owned the largest yacht in the world. Legend has it the Garner Mansion almost became the summer residence of Ulysses S. Grant and his wife, Julia. However, upon visiting it, his wife didn't like all the mosquitoes swarming the area and decided against it.

The home, located on the North Shore of Staten Island, is, according to the New York City Landmarks Preservation Commission, "one of the few freestanding pre–Civil War era mansions still surviving in New York City."

In the 1880s, the house became known first as St. Austin's Episcopal School for Boys and then later became St. Austin's Military Academy. It changed hands again in 1903, when the Sisters of Charity wanted to use the home as a facility for tuberculosis patients, but instead a general hospital was built for the community. An additional two-story frame structure, in the Colonial Revival style, was added at the rear of the original house. In 1906, the hospital opened it as a training school for nurses.

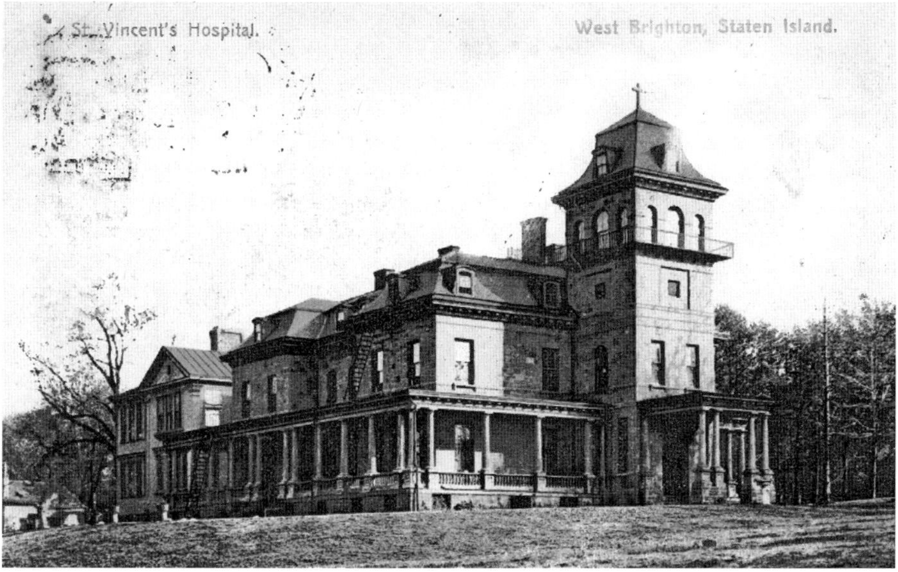

The former mansion of William T. and Mary Marcellite Garner became the site of Staten Island's St. Vincent's Hospital, founded by the Sisters of Charity in 1903. *Wikimedia Commons.*

This significant site, once the mansion of an 1800s millionaire, is the original home of St. Vincent's Hospital, one of Staten Island's first hospitals. Today, St. Vincent's Hospital is part of Richmond University Medical Center.

Chapter 8

Iconic Artistic Residents

Thespians

Buffalo Bill

When William F. Cody (1846–1917), better known as Buffalo Bill, ran a Wild West show that was the ultimate in Americana, full of cowboys and Mexicans and Native Americans as it was, more than half of New York City's entire population traveled to Staten Island to see it, according to the New York Public Library.

"In 1886, the Wild West came to the Mariners' Harbor (on Staten Island) and one to two million from the New York Metropolitan area followed. That's about one half to all of the New York City metropolitan area population at the time. The modern equivalent would be about 10 to 20 million people," according to NYPL.org. The shows not only changed Staten Island, but they also helped save the buffalo from extinction.

The story starts with Staten Island entrepreneur Erastus Wiman, according to the library:

> *He was a partner in the Wall Street investment firm Dun and Wiman and head of the Staten Island ferry and railroad companies. One day in 1885, Wiman had a somewhat scruffy looking visitor arrive unannounced at his Staten Island office. It was John Burke, general manager of Buffalo Bill's Wild West Co. Burke introduced himself:*

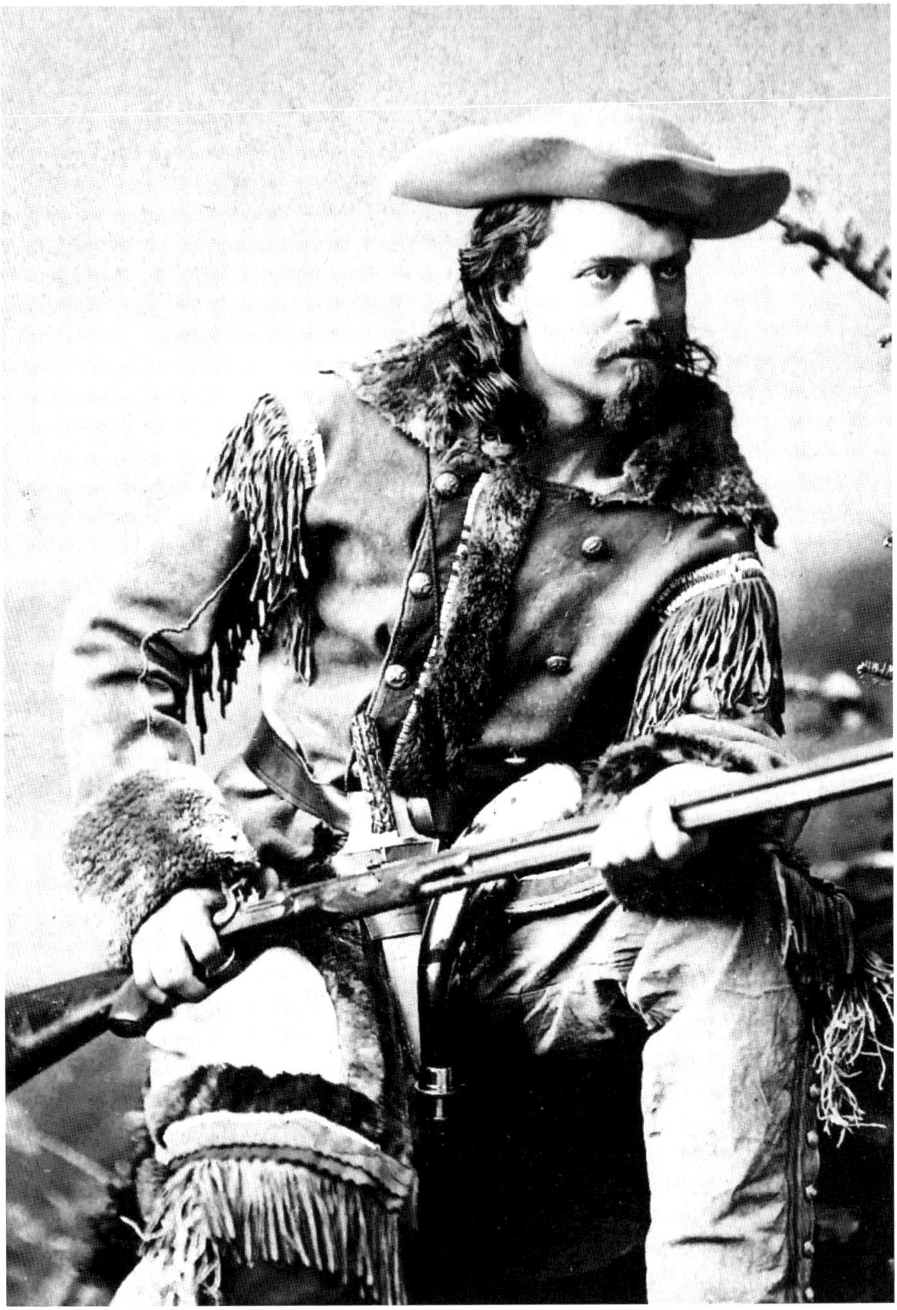

William F. Cody, aka Buffalo Bill. *Wikimedia Commons.*

> *"I have come all the way from Omaha, Mr. Wiman, to see you, and I hope you will not leave town without letting me have a few words..."*

Pulling out a newspaper clipping from Nebraska, he continued. He had a plan for great Staten Island tourist attractions, including baseball, huge stage shows and restaurants. All he needed was Wiman's ferry service and railroad. The project reminds one of the enormous redevelopment along Staten Island's North Shore in current times.

"I have been sent on to discover what are the chances for an alliance with the new Rapid Transit movement on Staten Island," said Burke, according to the NYPL, "and I want to secure your influence and energy in promoting our show at some good point on Staten Island."

The men took a carriage out to an undeveloped tract of land in Mariners' Harbor on the North Shore and planned to build the facilities needed. It is believed that Cody, Buffalo Bill himself, named the place "Erastina." The baseball stadium was also erected and gardens were planted and restaurants set up. A train line that was dubbed the "Buffalo Bill Express" ran four miles between the baseball stadium and Erastina along the North Shore starting in 1886.

In his book *Story of the Wild West and Camp-fire Chats*, Buffalo Bill recounted his arrival on Staten Island:

> *The harbor has probably never known a more picturesque scene than was witnessed yesterday morning, when the* Persian Monarch *steamed up from Quarantine, with Buffalo Bill standing on the captain's bridge, his tall and striking figure clearly outlined and his long hair waving in the wind, with the gaily painted and blanketed Indians leaning over the ship's rail, with the flags of all nations fluttering from the masts and connecting cables, and the band playing "Yankee Doodle" with a vim and enthusiasm which faintly indicated the joy felt by everybody connected with the Wild West exhibition, including the musicians, over the sight of home. The stolid Indians had lost their stolidity, and the white men on board declared that from the time the rising sun had enabled the redskins to discover America, or that part of it known as Staten Island, unwanted bustle and excitement had reigned supreme.*

He said that Native Americans such as Cut Meat, American Bear, Flat Iron, Tall Horse, Kills Plenty and dozens of fellow chiefs, braves and squaws

> *hugged the ship's side and watched every movement of the accompanying tugs until the great vessel was towed up alongside the long wharf at Tom*[p]*kinsville, and the huzzas of two thousand small boys and the noisy excitement of what seemed to be Staten Island's entire population. And it was a great day for Staten Island. So far as is known the* Persian Monarch *is the first great ocean steamer which has ever landed there, and this, taken in connection with the unusual nature of her passengers and her cargo, furnished abundant reason for the greatest possible commotion, excitement and disturbance whereof Mr. Wiman's small kingdom is capable.*

He continued to describe that

> *all the teamsters for miles around had been engaged to carry the outfit of the exhibition and of the exhibitors across the island to Erastina, and the wharf was in consequence a confused commingling of express wagons, butcher carts, carpenter's wagons and other kinds of vehicles, with horses attached generally on their haunches, in response to the excited demands of vociferous drivers. If this scene needed any further animation it was provided by the small boys dodging imminent death, and scores of pretty girls in their Sunday best, scurrying away from out the reach of the horses' indiscriminate hoofs.*

The Wild West show played here for six weeks before continuing on to Philadelphia, Baltimore, Washington and Richmond, Virginia. After Buffalo Bill left town, the Erastina grounds were home to small church and club picnics for a few years. Then in 1892, like so much of the land on Staten Island, the site was subdivided and sold off.

Mabel Normand

One of the earliest pioneers of cinema in the silent era was a tiny rebel with a heart of gold: Mabel Normand, born in New Brighton in 1892. In her brief but shining heyday, the diminutive five-foot-tall brunette beauty with enormous, expressive eyes was known alternately as the "Queen of Comedy" and the "Female Chaplin," according to *Mabel Normand: A Source Book to Her Life and Films* by William Thomas Sherman.

"Although for a while she was among the most favorite and praised of film stars, in about the mid 1920's that career took a pronounced downward turn due to unjustified and, to some extent, malicious scandal being leveled against her. So that it was not until a much later date (and aside from direct and indirect memorializing of her by Mack Sennett and associates), starting about the 1960's, that film historians began taking and evaluating the role she played and her work much more seriously," Sherman writes.

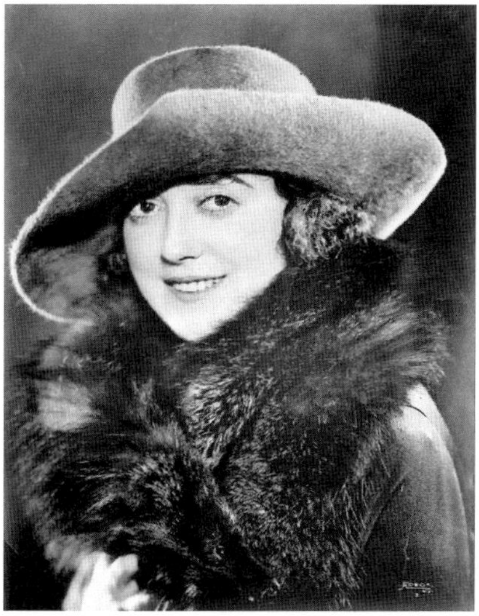

Silent film star Mabel Normand. *New York Public Library Collection.*

Mabel's films were made in the earliest days of Hollywood, and there were far fewer stars on the scene, so her legend was enormous. Since the films were silent, they could be understood more easily around the world; her reach was truly international.

"Further, she took on this new mantle with an independent mindedness and creative self-awareness relatively rare among her contemporaries," Sherman writes. "Indeed, when it came to bucking stiff convention and bypassing bland conformity, it would be no exaggeration to characterize her as one of Hollywood's very first rebels, yet a rebel very much with a heart, not to mention a warm and credible sense of humor."

Raised Catholic, she worked in the Butterick garment factory before taking up modeling, including for Charles Dana Gibson, creator of the "Gibson Girl," and regularly commuted via the Staten Island Ferry to her photo shoots.

In 1924, she said, "Up to the time I left school there was nothing eventful or particularly interesting in my life. My mother lived on Staten Island and I attended school, the last few years, at North Westport, Mass., near Martha's Vineyard. Once a month I went home…but I stayed at school, during the summer, studying hard and trying to skip a class and get ahead faster. I was tremendously ambitious in those days. We had very little money and even my occasional trips home were a great expense," according to Sherman's volume.

It wasn't long before she was discovered by Mack Sennett's Keystone Studios. She started as a bathing beauty, until Sennett noticed her comedic flair and began casting her as a featured actor in his popular short films.

"In 1914 she starred with Chaplin in what is considered to be the first feature length comedy, *Tillie's Punctured Romance* and became an international star," says Sherman.

Unfortunately, scandals rocked Hollywood from the start, and Mabel became associated with two murder cases in the 1920s, though she was innocent of any wrongdoing. In the first, her dear friend director William Desmond was killed in 1922 moments after she departed his home. "She was closely scrutinized by police but never considered a serious suspect," Sherman explains. Then, in 1924, her chauffeur, Joe Kelly, shot and wounded millionaire oil broker Courtland S. Dines with her pistol. Sherman wrote:

> *Newspapers speculated wildly about Normand given reports of her drug use along with her many past appearances in films with Roscoe "Fatty" Arbuckle who had also recently become enmeshed in scandal in which he was accused of raping and killing a young starlet (Virginia Rappe) during a wild multi-day party in his hotel suite. Arbuckle was later found innocent but the excesses of the stars of "Hollywood Babylon" resulted in a public backlash that would hamper or destroy the careers of the stars caught up in scandals that were damaging to the studios for which they worked. Even the great Chaplin would fall victim to scandals involving under aged girls that would culminate in a paternity suit that irrevocably damaged his public image. (Chaplin was not in fact the father of the child but was found guilty despite blood tests proving this).*

Though Mabel was not blacklisted, her career was never the same. Though she made more films for Hal Roach (also known for "Laurel and Hardy" and "Our Gang") and went on to marry fellow actor Lew Cody, her health took a downturn. Mabel died from tuberculosis in 1930 at the young age of thirty-seven.

"To say that Mabel was beautiful, vivacious and talented only hints at the amazing person that she was," according to the blog Comic Book Jones. "Normand was not only a major comedy star who worked along such legends as Chaplin, Arbuckle and Sennett, she was also a writer, director, producer and even ran her own production company for a time. It was a lesser feat for a man to walk on the moon than for a woman to be so influential in the early part of the twentieth century."

Maurice Barrymore

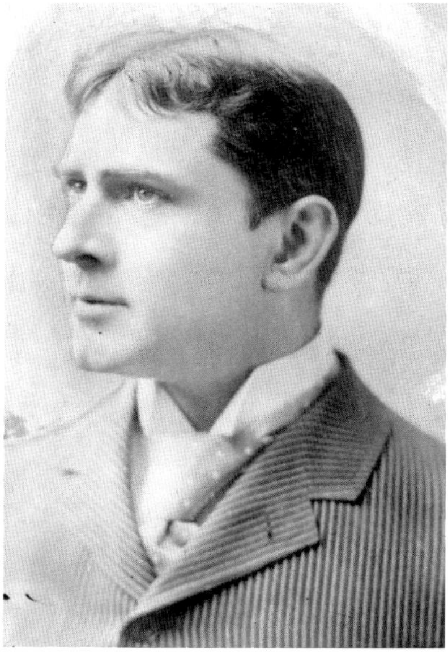

Maurice Barrymore, patriarch of the legendary Barrymore theatrical family. *Wikimedia Commons.*

The patriarch of the great Barrymore theatrical family—contemporary actor Drew Barrymore's great-grandfather Maurice—was born Herbert Arthur Chamberlayne Blythe in 1847 as a British citizen in Agra, India, not far from the Taj Mahal. He is famous locally for keeping exotic animals on a farm here in the nineteenth century.

His family, respectable British bureaucrats (his father was a surveyor for the East India Company), expected him to become an attorney, but he preferred boxing and the stage. When the call of the theater became too strong to ignore, his family begged him to at least change his name. He opened a book and pointed to the first character name he could find, and the rest was history.

"Though never a star, Barrymore was an excellent supporting actor and acted with many of the great names of theatre," according to Britannica. "He played with Augustin Daly's company, where he met Georgiana Drew, whom he married in 1876. He later joined Lester Wallack's company; on occasion he would be on the stage with his wife and son John. He took engagements in London and tried his hand at playwriting, with scant success, although (with much rewriting help) he did write original plays for Helena Modjeska and played in some of them."

While working in New York, the Barrymore clan—which now included wife Georgina Drew from another prominent acting family and their children Ethel, Lionel and John—would summer on Staten Island. The children would put on plays in the property's barn, charging a penny for admission.

True West magazine recounts one of the most legendary stories about the patriarch in which Barrymore led a theater troupe into Marshall, Texas, in 1879:

> *He and two associates were dining in the White House Saloon on the evening of March 19 when they were accosted by a drunken railroad man named Jim Currie. When Barrymore protested, Currie proceeded to kill one of the actors and put a bullet in Barrymore's chest.*
>
> *Barrymore somehow survived to act for another 20 years. Jim Currie—who apparently had important connections—was acquitted on grounds of temporary insanity.*

Barrymore's children succeeded beyond his own dreams. His eldest, Lionel (1878–1954), starred in Broadway plays such as *Peter Ibbetson* and *The Copperhead*. He then moved on to Hollywood and landed top roles in movies such as *A Free Soul* and *Grand Hotel*. Britannica describes him as a character actor who made two hundred films, including fifteen popular "Dr. Kildare" movies. Ethel Barrymore (1879–1959) appeared in London in *Peter the Great* and on Broadway in *Captain Jinks of the Horse Marines*. She opened the New York theater that now bears her name in 1928 in *The Kingdom of God* and later starred in *The Corn Is Green*. She appeared in more than thirty films, including *None but the Lonely Heart* and *The Spiral Staircase*. Their brother John Barrymore (1882–1942) was known for such plays as *Justice*, *Richard III* and especially *Hamlet*. His films include *Dr. Jekyll and Mr. Hyde* and *Dinner at Eight*.

Maurice Barrymore's great-granddaughter Drew Barrymore was born in 1975 and captured the world's hearts when she starred in Steven Spielberg's *E.T.* in 1982.

Martin Sheen

Martin Sheen is as well known for his sense of justice as for his star turns in classic films such as *Badlands* (1973) and *Apocalypse Now* (1979). Few people know he got his start on stage while working at the St. George Car Wash on Staten Island in the early 1960s, when, although self-taught, he was discovered by the founder of the Public Theater, Joseph Papp. It wouldn't be long until he was on his way, winning a Tony Award nomination for his role in *The Subject Was Roses* on Broadway in 1965. He would later return to Staten Island with colleagues Meryl Streep, Eric Bogosian and Mandy Patinkin to bury Papp in Baron Hirsch Cemetery in New Springville.

In the early years, Sheen lived in the Ambassador Building, an Art Deco apartment complex. In fact, his son Emilio Estevez was born on the living room floor there when they didn't get to the hospital in time.

He has been arrested many times for his activism against nuclear war, farmworkers' rights and other political hot buttons. When a bunch of swastikas were painted at his mentor Papp's Jewish cemetery, Sheen offered to make part of the rehabilitation of the young offenders a trip to Auschwitz in Poland to teach them a valuable lesson. The offenders were never caught.

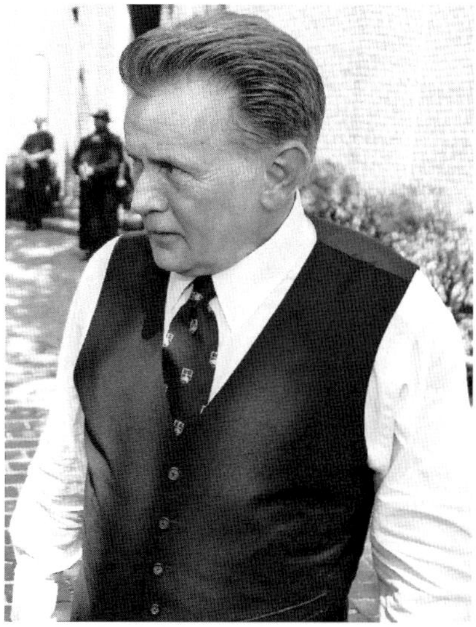

Actor and activist Martin Sheen. *Mayor Raymond L. Flynn records, Collection #0246.001, City of Boston Archives, Boston.*

A deeply spiritual man who took his stage name in honor of Catholic bishop Fulton J. Sheen, he came to New York with bus money lent to him by his own parish priest. He won many awards for his role as the Catholic president Josiah Bartlet on the TV series *The West Wing*. He also recently starred in the series *Grace and Frankie* on Netflix.

While filming *Apocalypse Now*, then thirty-eight-year-old Sheen had a heart attack. According to NNDB.com, "Over the next few years he reassessed his life, ending his use of drugs, cutting back on alcohol, and becoming much more politically active. He credits the guidance of longtime friend Terrence Malick for helping him find his way. In the years since, he has tended toward roles as leaders, often in films with a social statement to make."

Sheen wrote the foreword to the book *Broken and Shared: Food, Dignity and the Poor on Los Angeles' Skid Row* by Jeff Dietrich, and it offers good insight into his character:

> *Even for the most conservative among us there is little doubt that we are all responsible for each other, and the world is exactly the way it is because consciously, or unconsciously, we have made it so. But as things decline more and more rapidly with the world's economy in shambles, very few are aware of just how devastating the residual effects are on the poor who are ground down and served up daily to the gods of our idolatry: perpetual war, corporate greed, and personal indifference.*

According to Biography.com, he was born Ramon Estevez in Dayton, Ohio, in 1940 and recently celebrated his fiftieth wedding anniversary to Janet Templeton, with whom he has four children who are all actors: Emilio, Ramón, Carlos (Charlie Sheen) and Renée.

Robert Loggia

New Dorp High School graduate and Wagner College football player Salvatore "Robert" Loggia (1930–2015) had a successful career in Hollywood spanning sixty years. He was nominated for the Academy Award for Best Supporting Actor for *Jagged Edge* but is perhaps best remembered gliding along the electronic piano in FAO Schwartz opposite Tom Hanks in *Big*.

An army veteran who wrote for *Stars & Stripes*, Loggia could have succumbed to the mean streets of Staten Island as a young man on any number of occasions when tough guys would approach him. But he wanted to go to college and was destined for bigger, legitimate things. He enrolled with Stella Adler at the Actors Studio.

His acting credits are legion on both the big and small screens. In his first film in 1956, he undoubtedly drew from tough characters he knew in his youth and played a mobster opposite former fellow Staten Islander Paul Newman in *Somebody Up There Likes Me*, based on the life of boxer Rocky Graziano. He went on to do *The Greatest Story Ever Told* in 1965 and then *Revenge of the Pink Panther*, *An Officer and a Gentleman*, *Scarface*, *Prizzi's Honor*, *Independence Day*, *Lost Highway*, *Return to Me* and *Tim and Eric's Billion Dollar Movie*. On television, he was known for roles on the martial arts series *T.H.E. Cat* and hits like *Mancuso, FBI*; *Malcolm in the Middle*; *The Sopranos*; and *Men of a Certain Age*, according to the Internet Movie Database (IMDB). He even played Anwar Sadat opposite Ingrid Bergman's Golda Meir in the 1982 television movie *A Woman Called Golda*.

He relished the diversity of the roles he played and was once quoted as saying, "An actor is an impersonator; he plays many different roles. If you played the same role all the time, God—that'd be a boring career. When you take on different roles and become a different person, that's called acting… It's a challenge," according to BrainyQuote.com.

In 2010, Loggia was both honored with the Ellis Island Medal of Freedom and diagnosed with Alzheimer's disease.

In his *Los Angeles Times* obituary, Loggia was remembered as a tough guy with a soft side. "Often referred to as a tough guy, Loggia could be suave

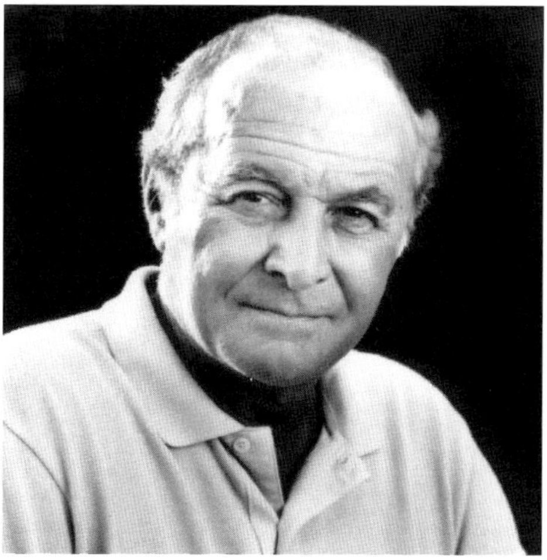

Actor Robert Loggia. *Wikimedia Commons.*

and tender. His voice could go raspy and then slip to silken. He was also playful. In *Big*, he and Hanks, a boy magically turned into a man, played 'Chopsticks' while dancing over large, lighted piano keys on the floor."

The paper said he excelled, however, "at playing men with rap sheets and unsettled demons. He appeared in *The Sopranos* as Michele 'Feech' La Manna, who sought his place back in the mob after a prison stint. He once summed up his talent as: 'I'm a character actor in that I play many different roles, and I'm virtually unrecognizable from one role to another. So I never wear out my welcome.'"

Variety quoted his widow, Audrey, upon his death a few years ago: "He loved being an actor. He used to say that he never had to work. He never had to wait tables."

Alyssa Milano

Actor Alyssa Milano was born in Bensonhurst, Brooklyn, in 1972, but a neighborhood shooting there inspired her family to move to Great Kills, Staten Island, in her early childhood.

Alyssa got her start when one of her babysitters took her to an audition without her parents' knowledge and she landed a role in the Broadway play *Annie*. She grew up before America's eyes, next portraying adorable Samantha Micelli on the hit TV series *Who's the Boss?* opposite Tony Danza. Unlike many child actors, she remains successful in adulthood and avoided many of the pitfalls.

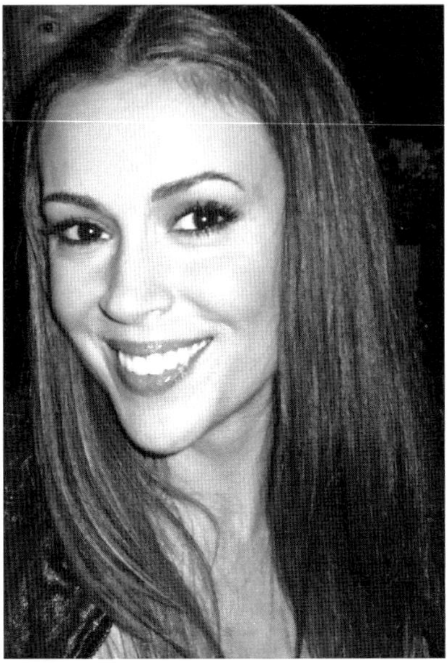

Alyssa Milano. *Wikimedia Commons.*

"Alyssa has a history of starring in long running successful television series. She starred on the hit WB series *Charmed* for nine years," according to her website, Alyssa.com. "The series' debut was the highest-rated premiere in the network's history, and continued to be a great success for Spelling and The WB. The show's international appeal has brought it to more than 100 territories around the world, spanning Europe, Asia, Africa and Australia. She also starred on the Fox cornerstone series *Melrose Place*....Alyssa also had a recurring role on the hit NBC comedy, *My Name Is Earl*, and starred in the ABC comedy, *Romantically Challenged*."

The beautiful brunette, who is married and has a son and a daughter, also has had success on the big screen. She appeared in Garry Marshall's *New Year's Eve*, with Robert DeNiro, Ashton Kutcher, Zac Efron, Michelle Pfeiffer, Hilary Swank and Sarah Jessica Parker; and *Hall Pass*, opposite Owen Wilson and Jason Sudeikis. Her film credits also include *Hugo Pool*, co-starring Sean Penn and Robert Downey Jr.; the Imagine/Universal film *Fear*; and *Dickie Roberts: Former Child Star*. She provided a lead voice for Disney's sequel to the animated favorite *Lady and the Tramp*. She was seen in Lifetime's *Sundays at Tiffany's*, based on the bestselling novel by James Patterson. Alyssa also played the title character in the Lifetime original movie *Wisegal* (which she also produced).

Milano was made a National Ambassador by UNICEF in 2003 and has traveled to Angola, India and beyond to raise awareness of children in crisis. Here in the United States, she has helped with the organization's big "Trick or Treat" Halloween philanthropic campaign as its spokesperson.

A huge baseball fan, her book *Safe at Home: Confessions of a Baseball Fanatic* was released in 2009. And her graphic novel, *Hacktivist*, is a critical success. She told *Maxim* magazine, "I grew up in a very creative family and I believe that has truly given me the base for many of my projects and passions. I like to find projects where I can break the stereotype of creators....*Hacktivist* is definitely one of those areas—as was my Touch Women's Sports Fashion Collection 8 years ago. And I love to work!"

She is currently hosting Lifetime's *Project Runway All Stars* with Isaac Mizrahi and Georgina Chapman.

Milano is very vocal on Twitter and frequently criticizes the Trump administration. She recently posted, "Those that tell me not to tweet politics because I'm an uninformed celebrity are the same people that voted for... an uninformed celebrity."

She also uses her Twitter platform to raise awareness of dyslexia, from which she suffers. "Milano is dyslexic, and for her, memorizing lines and reading scripts hasn't always come easy," according to Dyslexiahelp.com. "Though she struggled with reading early in her acting career, Milano credits British thespian Sir John Gielglud for helping her overcome her learning disability."

"When I asked him how he memorized his monologues, he said, 'I write them down,'" Milano is quoted by the website. "I use that method to this day. It not only familiarizes me with my words, it makes them my own."

Rick Schroder

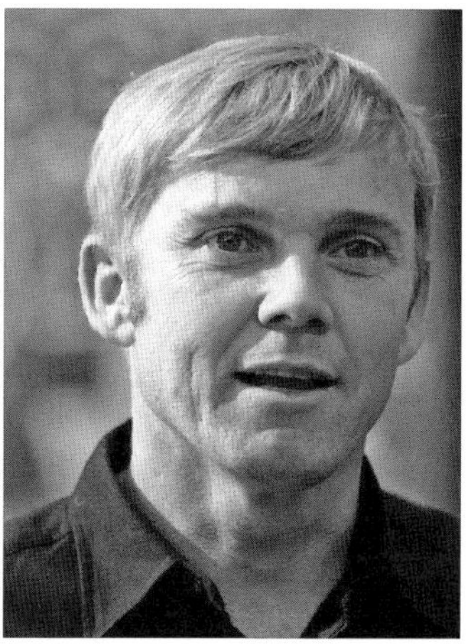

Actor Rick Schroder. *Wikimedia Commons.*

Rick Schroder was born in 1970 in Brooklyn and moved to Great Kills, Staten Island, with his family early in his childhood. Not long after that, he would steal the world's hearts playing Jon Voight's son in the 1979 film *The Champ*. He won the Golden Globe Award in 1980 for Best New Male Star of the Year in a Motion Picture for that role.

"For a child more used to stealing bases than scenes, Ricky Schroder should have felt bush league, all right, in the face of the star power assembled for his movie debut in *The Champ*," wrote *People* magazine at the time. "The actor playing Ricky's boxer dad (yes, this was a remake of the 1931 Jackie Cooper classic) was Jon Voight, in his first part since his Oscar-winning *Coming Home*. Another Oscar laureate, Faye Dunaway (*Network*), had the female lead. The director was Italian Franco

Zeffirelli, a veteran of films with the likes of Richard Burton and Sir Alec Guinness."

All that would have daunted most kids, *People* pointed out, "but the towheaded Schroder, who turned 9 last month, made out like a thief anyway. Thanks largely to his cry-on-cue ability, *The Champ* milks more emotion out of its weepy plot than any pug epic since *Rocky*. More remarkable, Ricky managed both to impress critics and to leave his upstaged co-stars with feelings of genuine affection."

Lightning would strike twice when Schroder was cast in the hit series *Silver Spoons* at the age of twelve, catapulting him to heartthrob status.

Talking to Oprah on her OWN Network a few years ago, he said:

> *The whole thing with the screaming girls and stuff, I didn't understand....*
>
> *It is a challenge transitioning from a child star, because if your ego is totally tied up in your work and if you don't work for a while, it can be scary. It's very hard to have been famous and try to live a normal life—like Gary Coleman did, for example. I knew Gary and he was a good guy. And he had some challenges in life and he overcame them, and I admired him for that. But he just didn't transition. And I always felt sympathy for Gary, what it felt like to be Gary as a security guard. It's almost cruel.*

Schroder married at twenty and started a family, and he credited feeling grounded in that with his later success. He starred in the successful mini-series *Lonesome Dove* and TV crime drama *NYPD Blue*. "I just had that kind of tenacious attitude to not quit," he told Oprah. "And also there were opportunities for me when I needed them."

Glamour magazine asked him recently about his role as Danny Sorenson on the hit series *NYPD Blue*, and he said it was one of the most challenging of his career:

> *It was really like acting boot camp for me. I'd never had people be so demanding in a good way, of me, than the executives of* NYPD Blue. *The directors, the producers, they were so demanding, as well as the fellow cast members because the show was cutting edge for its time. I would come to work sometimes, and there would be no script.* [Co-creator and head writer] *David Milch was notorious for that. He would write in the moment, so we would show up to work and have no dialogue, and then all of a sudden, it's 6:30 or 7 in the morning, it's time to rehearse, and David shows up and hands you four or five pages. The dialogue had its own*

> *rhythm, and it was unique, so you had to learn that and be ready to shoot it in like, 90 minutes, while you're getting wardrobe and getting ready to go. It was challenging. But it made me a better actor, that show. It made me appreciate my fellow actors more. It was just boot camp for me, acting boot camp. Loved every minute of it. And very proud of what we accomplished.*

Rick's wife, Andrea Schroder, filed for divorce in 2016. The couple have four children together.

George M. Cohan

The Broadway impresario who composed some of our nation's most patriotic songs, from "You're a Grand Old Flag" to "Over There" to "Yankee Doodle Boy," lived in the Actor's Home in West Brighton, Staten Island, for a time.

He was born in 1878 in Providence, Rhode Island, to veteran vaudeville troupers Jeremiah and Helen Costigan Cohan. It wouldn't be long before George and his sister Josephine would join the act, known as the Four Cohans. The family toured from coast to coast across America. He began playing the violin and later dancing. It wasn't long before he landed his first starring role in *Peck's Bad Boy*.

A prolific composer and vaudeville sketch writer said to have created 150 works between the ages of seventeen and twenty-one, Cohan's genius lay in how he chose to get paid. "In these he laid the foundation for his fortune," according to the *New York Times*, "as he did not sell them for the standard rate of $50 each, but insisted on royalties of $10 to $25 a week on each sketch as long it was played."

In 1901 he wrote, composed, directed and produced *The Governor's Son*, his first Broadway production, which took the Four Cohans into the legitimate theater. Soon thereafter, at the age of twenty-six, he joined forces with another young man, Sam H. Harris, in a partnership that took Broadway by storm and made reputation and riches for both. Together they put on *Little Johnny Jones*, a patriotic production toward which the orthodox dramatic critics were cool but that became one of Broadway's greatest hits.

In his *New York Times* obituary in 1942, Cohan was hailed as one of the all-time greats of the theater:

> *George M. Cohan called himself "just a song-and-dance man," but at the height of his career he was unquestionably the first man in the American*

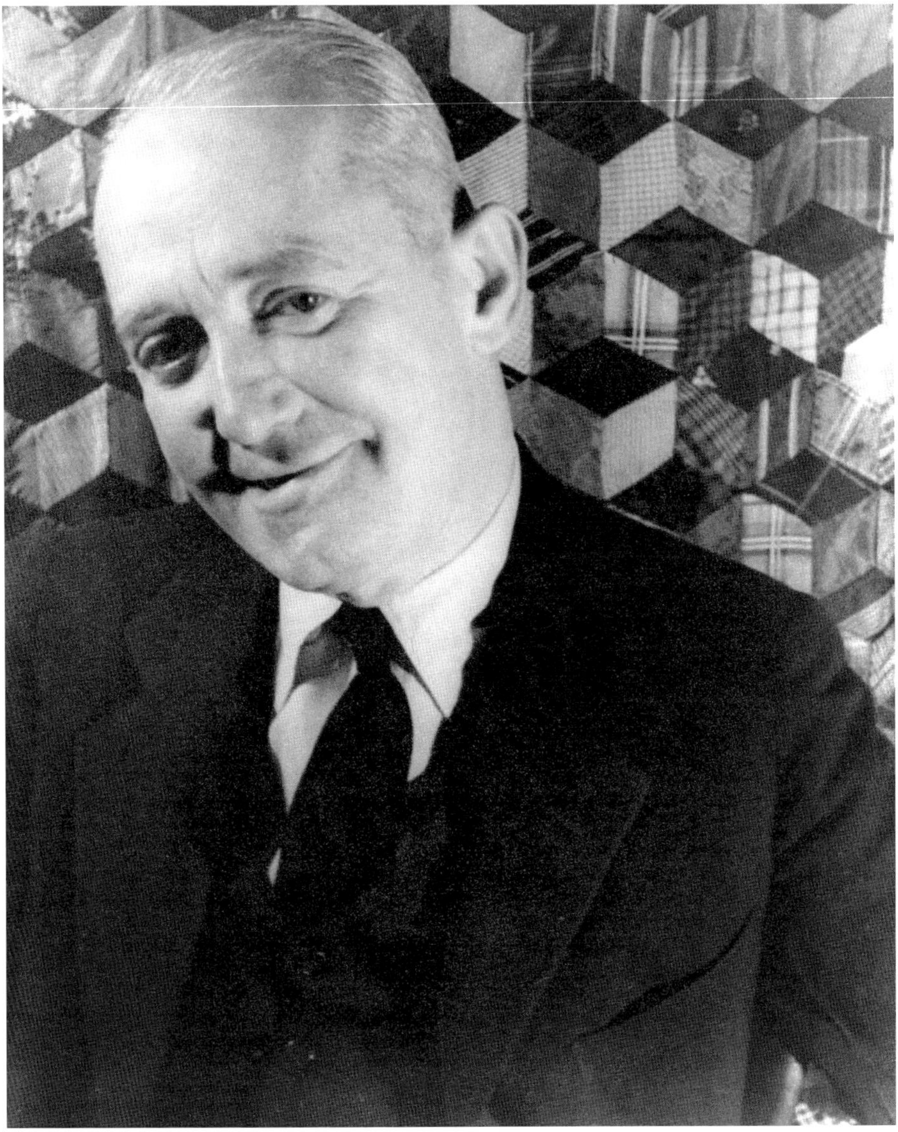

George M. Cohan, Broadway impresario and patriotic composer. *Library of Congress.*

theatre. Songwriter, dancer, actor, playwright, producer, theatre owner—he was the most versatile person in show business. An old trouper and hoofer, whose dapper costumes, derby or straw hat cocked jauntily over one eye, wisecracks from the corner of the mouth, and lively caper across the stage with his fast-swinging cane, were nationally known trademarks, he was

> *regarded for years as just a Broadway vaudeville performer, but astonished the theatrical world by developing into a serious actor and dramatist whose work won praise even from the intellectuals who had previously ignored him. Born and raised in the theatre, he could give lessons to the most erudite of university men in its technique.*

Cohan was incredibly philanthropic. The *Times* states that "Over There" sold more than 1,500,000 copies, and Cohan received $25,000 for the mechanical instrument rights alone, "which he gave to his mother, who distributed it among soldiers' funds and civic charities. He joined an all-star cast in 1918 which made a two-week tour in a war play called *Out There*." This grossed $600,000 for the Red Cross."

When *Yankee Doodle Dandy* made it to Hollywood starring James Cagney in the story of Cohan's life, he encouraged premiere-goers and others to buy war bonds. More than $5 million was raised.

Perhaps President Franklin Delano Roosevelt said it best in his telegram to Cohan's widow. Quoted by the *Times*, it read: "A beloved figure is lost to our national life in the passing of your devoted husband. He will be mourned by millions whose lives were brightened and whose burdens were eased by his genius as a fun maker and as a dispeller of gloom. My heartfelt sympathy to you and all the family."

MUSICIANS

Jenny Lind

No recordings of the legendary opera singer Jenny Lind (1820–1887) survive, but hers must have been quite a voice indeed, as she was called the "Swedish Nightingale" for her gorgeous and complex intonations, known as "coloratura." Lind was a famous soprano by age eleven in Europe after being discovered singing by a maid to the principal dancer at the Royal Swedish Opera, according to the Oxford Dictionary of National Biography. The maid fetched her employer, who listened with amazement at the young girl's voice. With her help, Jenny Lind was granted an audition and enrolled in the Royal Dramatic Theater.

Her voice was fine but fragile, and she had to be rehabilitated by voice coaches and doctors a couple of times. "By the time Lind was 28, she was already set to retire from the operatic stage," according to a recent article by Smithsonian. "The audience for Lind's farewell performance included Queen Victoria, who presented the singer with a gem-encrusted nightingale. While she was the darling of Europe, in 1849 almost no one in the United States knew who Lind was."

Then in 1850, she was invited to America to tour by showman P.T. Barnum. She earned $350,000 and used it to fulfill her dream of founding a music conservatory for girls in Sweden.

According to Smithsonian, Barnum had not even heard Lind sing until the first night of the tour in New York City. But that didn't stop the legendary showman from creating lots of hype. "Barnum published several announcements of Lind's arrival in newspapers, advertising the singer's philanthropic nature." Barnum staged events like auctions of tickets to Lind's concerts, "which drove up the price from an average of $6.38 per ticket to over $200 for Lind's New York debut," Smithsonian states. "The showman even held a poetic competition, which would furnish the lyrics for a new song that Lind would sing throughout her tour."

The Lost Museum blog of the City University of New York (CUNY) says that in Lind, Barnum created the first true star. "Barnum succeeded in building such great public anticipation about the 'Swedish Nightingale' that forty thousand people showed up to greet the arrival of her ship in New York harbor." From her opening concert in New York City's Castle Garden to subsequent performances in cities and towns across the country, Barnum fueled public fascination with Lind by orchestrating events and negotiating Lind-endorsed products (including Jenny Lind songs, clothes, chairs and pianos). "Lindomania" lasted until 1852, when the partnership collapsed over logistical and financial issues. Barnum shrewdly promoted Lind's character—her modesty, benevolence and selflessness—as much as her artistry. One scholar contends that because of Barnum's promotion, Lind became "the standard for measuring not just sopranos, or even women artists, but women" throughout the 1850s, according to CUNY.

Such was the excitement that "there were reports that hotel maids were selling Lind's hair after stealing it from the singer's brush, and that men were kissing gloves Lind threw out to the crowd. Promotional and souvenir consumer products contributed to 'Lindomania,' as Jenny Lind gloves, bonnets, hats, shawls, chairs, pianos, cigars, and even paper dolls were sold throughout the country," according to Smithsonian.

During her time in the United States, she lived for two years in West Brighton, performing many concerts at the Pavilion Hotel there, according

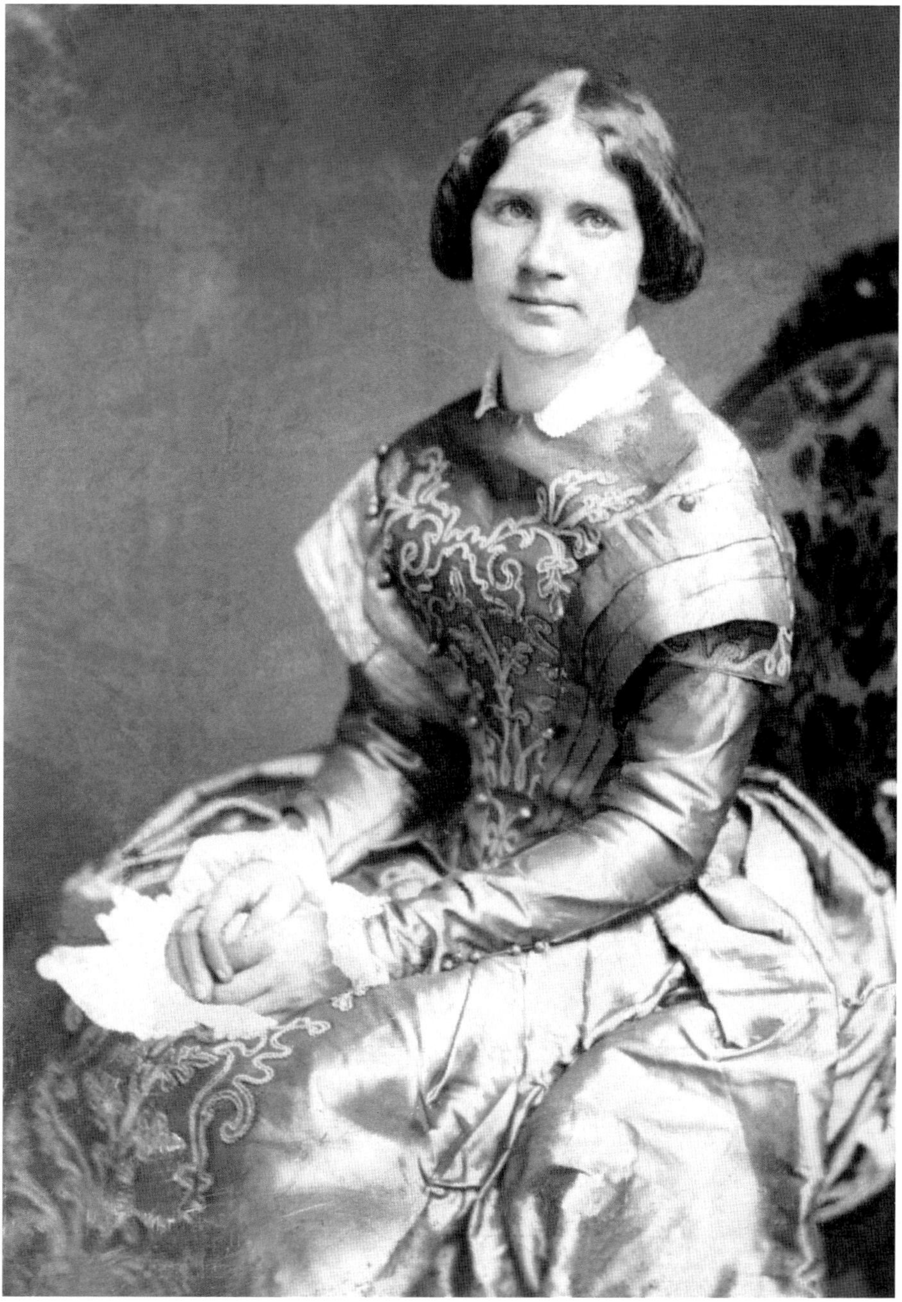

"The Swedish Nightingale," Jenny Lind, opera star. *Wikimedia Commons.*

to Thomas W. Matteo, EdD, and Margaret Lundrigan, PsyD, in their book *Legendary Locals of Staten Island*.

"She received her first bouquet in America from the writer and abolitionist George William Curtis (for whom Curtis High School here is named) after a performance at Castle Garden Opera," Matteo and Lundrigan state.

Roy Clark

Most people know country legend Roy Clark (born in 1933), who lived in Great Kills on Staten Island during his childhood, for starring in the guffaw-filled variety show *Hee Haw* for over two decades. His character on that show—seen by thirty million viewers weekly in its heyday—unfortunately is but a caricature of the man. In fact, he is a virtuoso guitar player respected by many greats across musical genres. One need only listen to his version of the Spanish guitar classic "Malaguena" to get a sense of his enormous talent.

Clark and his family moved to the South Shore of Staten Island from Virginia when his father took a job with the Baltimore and Ohio Railroad here in the late 1930s. Times were hard, and when his father lost that job, Roy Clark remembers loading up whatever family possessions could fit in the back of their truck and heading back to Virginia.

The young man who practiced his trade on the Staten Island Ferry ended up having better luck: he won two national banjo competitions in his teens that changed his life. Soon he was among the giants of the country music industry, having earned an appearance at the Grand Ole Opry in Nashville, Tennessee.

"I stood backstage…and looked at Uncle Dave Macon, Hank Williams, Sr., Cowboy Copas—all of the giants of country music—and I just tried to stay out of their way," Roy said in a report published by the Opry. Clark ended up touring with Opry legends Stringbean and Grandpa Jones, according to the report. He next backed up Red Foley and Ernest Tubb.

"A virtuoso on all stringed instruments, he also could handle trombone, trumpet and piano to boot," says the Opry. "Roy's guitar wizardry garnered him his first serious notice, at age 27. An invitation to open for Wanda Jackson led to his own tour, for 365 straight nights, and a trip to Las Vegas as a headliner. The next year he had his first hit, 'Tips of My Fingers,' a Bill Anderson–penned country song with orchestra and strings."

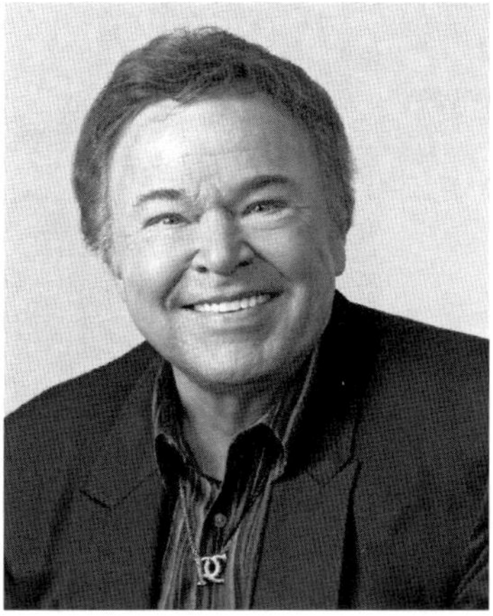

Country legend Roy Clark. *Official publicity photo.*

Roy Clark crossed over to popular music beginning in the 1960s with hits like "Yesterday, When I Was Young," "Thank God and Greyhound" and "Wichita Lineman." He became a popular guest on *The Tonight Show with Johnny Carson*, as well as *The Flip Wilson Show* and *The Mike Douglas Show*.

He has won the industry's highest awards, such as the Country Music Association's (CMA) Entertainer and Instrumentalist of the Year and the Instrumental Group of the Year category with Buck Trent. The Academy of Country Music has honored him for the following categories: Comedy Act, Lead Guitar and Entertainer of the Year. He is perhaps proudest of his Pioneer Award with the organization. Roy Clark has a star on Hollywood's Walk of Fame and won a Grammy in 1982 for *Alabama Jubilee*.

Clark is also credited with creating country music mecca Branson, Missouri, by opening the Roy Clark Celebrity Theater there in 1983.

Clark has lived in Tulsa, Oklahoma, since 1974 and still keeps a full concert schedule. He took a break for ten years starting in 2000 but returned with the recording titled *Christmas Memories* and two gospel albums.

In 2009, Roy Clark was inducted into the Country Music Hall of Fame.

He has been married to his wife, Barbara, with whom he has four children, since 1957. In Tulsa, there is an elementary school named for him.

David Johansen

David Johansen of West Brighton, born in 1950 here to a Norwegian tenor and a New York Irish librarian who met while working in Barnes & Noble, fronted the proto-punk band New York Dolls in the 1970s with flamboyant glam-/glitter-rock makeup and outfits, influencing a generation. Staten Islanders delight in seeing this favorite son out and about in the borough, and sightings range from CVS to Girardi's Farmers Market.

The family lived in a housing project until David was six, he said in an interview with the UK's *Independent*. When they got into their first

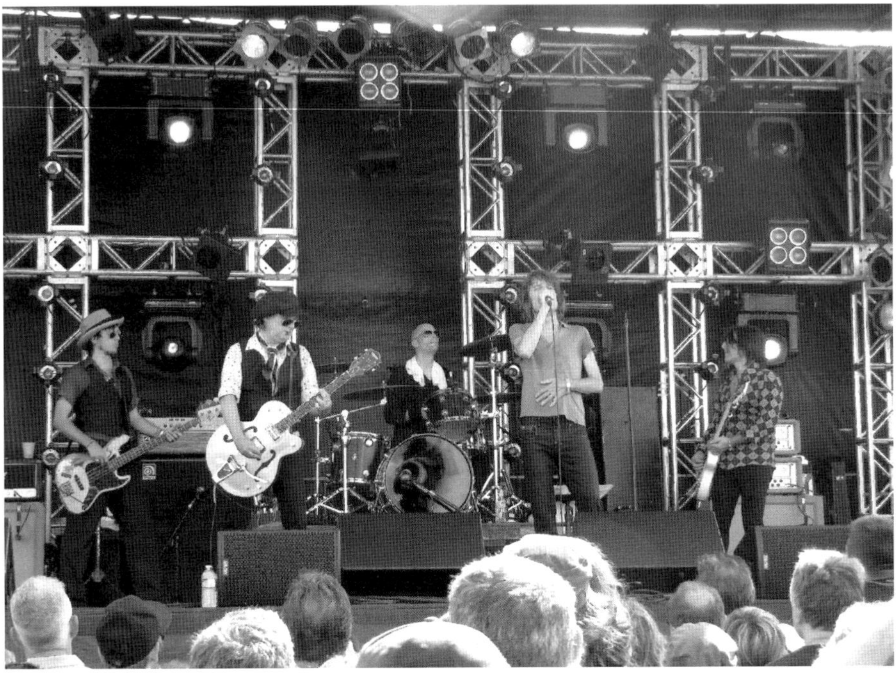

Rock star David Johansen. *Wikimedia Commons.*

house, there were colorful people next door, he told them. "There was this place next door to my mother's house; when I was about eight years old all the members of the alcoholic family who lived there died in quick succession. I managed to get inside and discovered hundreds of empty bottles in the basement and made a concoction out of the dregs. I'll never forget that place."

A thoughtful and well-read intellectual, Johansen's childhood curiosity has led to him trying on many personas. "David Johansen was a true chameleon; throughout the course of a career which saw him transform from a lipstick-smeared proto-punk hero into an urbane blue-eyed soul man and finally into a tuxedo-clad lounge lizard, he remained a rock & roll original, an unpredictable iconoclast and a true cultural innovator," according to *Billboard* magazine.

Johansen has been a musician since his teens, joining the Vagabond Missionaries and Fast Eddie & the Electric Japs before he met bassist Arthur Kane, who extended an invitation to join his band, Actress, according to *Billboard*. "After changing their name to the New York Dolls, the group began building a notorious reputation for their menacing, edgy music, drug-fueled lifestyle, and outrageously campy, drag queen–inspired glam image; although neither their eponymous 1973 debut nor 1974's *Too Much Too Soon* even cracked the Top 100, the Dolls established an enduring cult following, and their influence on the rise of punk was unmistakable."

In the late 1980s, Johansen came up with an alter ego known as Buster Poindexter, a musicologist and lounge lizard. The incredibly liberating persona with a pompadour allowed Johansen to explore all types of music. He began touring with a big band called the Banshees in Blue, and they were a hit everywhere they played. When they released an album called *Buster Poindexter* in 1987, the breakout hit from the album was "Hot, Hot, Hot," which was his first big commercial success but also "the bane of my existence," as he is frequently quoted.

"As Poindexter, he resuscitated the lounge music genre that, while popular in the '50s and '60s, had come to be seen as passé, and refashioned it into a vehicle for his over-the-top-personality," according to *Interview* magazine. "With his big, carefully arranged hair, glittery tuxedos and formal wear, and exaggerated singing style he became a crooner."

Johansen revived the Buster character for the albums *Buster Goes Berserk* in 1989 and *Buster's Happy Hour* in 1994. He then went into quiet reflection, only to reappear as a folk singer with the release of *David Johansen & the Harry Smiths* in 2000. He now hosts *David Johansen's Mansion of Fun*, a weekly show on Sirius Satellite Radio.

Christina Aguilera

Christina Aguilera was born in Staten Island University Hospital in December 1980 and lived in Grasmere in her early childhood before moving to a Pittsburgh suburb and on to superstardom. Though most of her family moved on, her paternal grandparents, Ecuadorian immigrants Fausto and Edna Aguilera of Rosebank—a navy veteran and steamship captain and family matriarch, respectively—lived here until they both passed away in 2015.

She was discovered at just eight years old when she appeared on *Star Search*, earning a spot on the *New Mickey Mouse Club* with fellow budding stars like Britney Spears and Justin Timberlake. Her stunning soprano falsetto graced the soundtrack of Disney's *Mulan* with "Reflection" in 1998, and she went on to hits like "Genie in a Bottle" and "What a Girl Wants" before winning a Grammy Award for Best New Artist in 2000. She has won four more since then.

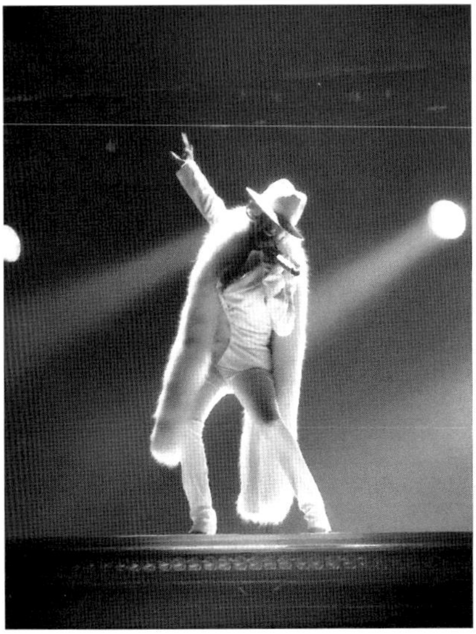

Singer and *The Voice* judge Christina Aguilera. *Wikimedia Commons.*

Far more than the "Pop Princess" title she earned early on, Aguilera's voice is one of the finest in the industry, on par with Mariah Carey, Whitney Houston and Barbra Streisand. "Aguilera has been one of the foremost practitioners of the overpowering, Category 5 vocal style known as melisma," David Browne wrote in the *New York Times*. According to Dictionary.com, melisma is "an expressive vocal phrase or passage consisting of several notes sung to one syllable."

And Sasha Frere-Jones wrote in the *New Yorker*, "Aguilera doesn't need to reincarnate Sarah Vaughan to be a serious singer. She already is one, in the tradition of nineteen-nineties pop and R&B, skillfully deploying melisma for razzle-dazzle."

Aguilera has been vocal about violence in her early home, with both she and her mother accusing her father of being abusive. (He denied the allegations.) Her parents divorced when she was six years old.

She has also raised the subject of bullying and says she channels the pain of all those experiences into her songs. In an interview with E!, she said, "Growing up I did not feel safe. Feeling powerless is the worst feeling in the world. I turned to singing as an outlet. The pain at home is where my love for music came from."

In an interview with *Dateline NBC*, she addressed bullying. "I have definitely experienced forms of bullying, and that's why it's so important for me to write songs like 'Beautiful' and 'Fighter.' On this current record, 'Lotus' is all about being an unbreakable flower that survives the test of time. Throughout the roughest of surroundings and harshest weather conditions it remains strong and thrives."

She has been a coach on *The Voice* for six seasons and is currently being recruited by *America's Got Talent*.

The Wu-Tang Clan

The Wu-Tang Clan is one of the most successful creative collectives in the history of music. As a pioneer of the hip-hop industry, the Wu-Tang Clan has successfully created its own niche in a competitive genre. Its music, its message and its loyalty among its fan base have spanned the course of over two decades and are unparalleled.

After the release of its single "Protect Ya Neck" in 1993, the Wu-Tang Clan became a successful and widely popular hip-hop rap group. By the time it completed touring with the rap groups Cypress Hill and Kat Nu, the Wu-Tang Clan had a legion of fans and a cult-like following. As a result of such resounding success, the Wu-Tang Clan signed a record deal with the label Loud/RCA. The business deal allowed the Wu-Tang Clan to record as a rap group, yet it also afforded its members the opportunity to record their own solo albums if they desired.

With the success of its debut album, *Enter the Wu-Tang (36 Chambers)*, the group went on to enjoy critical acclaim; according to rocklistmusic.co.uk,

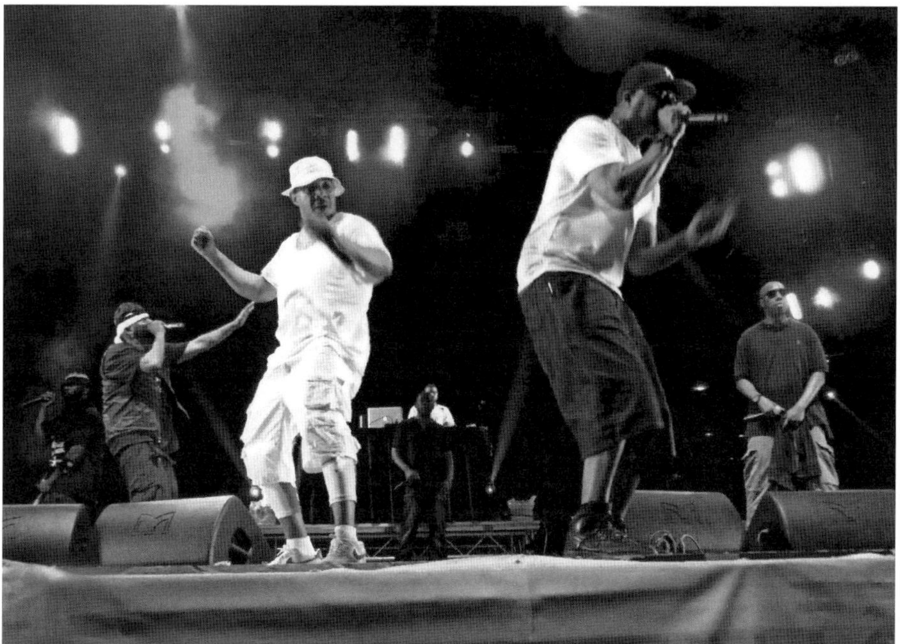

The Wu-Tang Clan, performing in Budapest Park, Budapest, 2015. *Wikimedia Commons.*

its debut album is regarded as one of the greatest hip-hop rap albums of all time.

The nine original members of the group were raised on the Borough of Staten Island in the 1970s and '80s, where they grew up living in the tenement projects in some of Staten Island's poorest and toughest inner-city neighborhoods. The group's lyrics often highlight its affinity for kung fu movies, the Chinese dynasty, samurai warriors and kung fu weapons, and the group often refers to itself as the Wu-Tang Killa Beez. Most of its poignant lyrics mention the challenges and struggles of a poor life on the streets of Staten Island, or, as the group says, "the streets of 'Shaolin.'" Shaolin is actually the name of a Chinese Buddhist monastery; however, the Wu-Tang Clan uses the word "Shaolin" in many of its songs as a nickname for its hometown of Staten Island. There, in this New York City borough, is where the group's dynasty was born and its rap sound perfected, according to Ryan Beagle's 2016 article "Top 5 Rappers from Staten Island" on hiphopgoldenage.com. As a result of the several references to Staten Island in the Wu-Tang Clan's countless songs spanning five albums, many of the group's fans have come to know the Borough of Staten Island affectionately as Shaolin. That the group calls its hometown "Shaolin" is quoted in one of their tracks by Method Man:

> *From the slums of Shaolin, Wu-Tang Clan strikes again*
> *The RZA, the GZA, Ol Dirty Bastard, Inspectah Deck, Raekwon the Chef*
> *U-God, GhostFace Killah, and the Method Man*

Over the course of many years, the Wu-Tang Clan grew in numbers by collaborating with up-and-coming rap artists, providing them with a platform to showcase their talent. Some of these artists, such as Busta Rhymes, Kanye West and MF Doom, went on to achieve success in the music industry as influential solo rap artists. Furthermore, within the span of two decades, the Wu-Tang Clan has accrued a national and international fan base.

The business savvy of the Wu-Tang Clan enabled it to reach popularity and profit outside the music industry. With such a tremendous following of loyal fans, the group capitalized on their success and their moniker. The original nine founding members were featured in a PlayStation video game in 1999 called *Wu-Tang: Shaolin Style*. The gaming system also offered for sale a special collector's edition controller. The group also had a clothing line of Wu Wear clothes in the early 1990s, and Wu Wear stores opened in New York City, Los Angeles, Atlanta and Virginia. According to Linda Hobbs's 2007 article "Vbeat: Clan in Da Front" in *Vibe* magazine, the clothing line yielded a profit of $10 million in 1998. Nike even produced a Wu-Tang Clan–themed Dunk High sneaker in the group's honor. It is also the subject of the 2007 documentary film *WU: The Story of the Wu-Tang Clan*. Moreover, the success of its adult books, *The Wu-Tang Manual* and *The Tao of Wu*, explained the group's lyrical philosophy. *The Wu-Tang Manual* laid out the intricate web of personalities (and alter egos), warrior codes, numerological systems and eastern spiritual ethics that define the Wu-Tang dynasty. *The Tao of Wu* continued the conversation with RZA, imparting the lessons he learned on his journey from the Staten Island projects to international superstardom.

The original nine members (and their alter egos) of the Wu-Tang Clan included:

RZA (Robert Fitzgerald Diggs, 1969), the self-proclaimed de facto leader of the group. He not only designed the Clan's copyrighted logo but also produced the entirety of their debut album, *Enter the Wu-Tang (36 Chambers)*. He is the leader of the Wu-Tang Clan and most recognized for creating the group's rhythmic beats and unique tracks on its albums. RZA is considered by many as a producing pioneer in the hip-hop music industry. His visionary talent remains unsurpassed, and he went on to produce many of the group's solo albums as well.

GZA (Gary Grice, 1966), the oldest founding member in the group. According to Kevin Beacham's 2005 article "Time Travelin' with the Genius" on ohword.com, GZA began rapping as far back as 1976, a time when hip-hop was considered a New York phenomenon with a serious underground following. Prior to GZA joining the Wu-Tang Clan, he had already recorded a solo album of his own called *Words from the Genius*. As one of the MCs of the group, GZA offers a "laid-back" flow, where lyrics, often referring to samurai films, are set in metaphors. After becoming an instrumental member of the Wu-Tang Clan, he went on to release another popular solo album, *Liquid Swords*.

Ol' Dirty Bastard, also known as ODB (Russell Tyrone Jones, 1968–2004). ODB was considered one of the group's most erratic and unstable members. His behavior garnered much media attention, as well as the attention of law enforcement officials. He spent several years incarcerated due to drug possession. ODB, considered one of the more popular members of the Clan, had an easily recognizable rapping style. His emphasized vocal inflections embedded within his offbeat rhymes were a fan favorite. In 2004, ODB collapsed while in the recording studio and was pronounced dead several days after. According to the 2004 article "Ol' Dirty Bastard—Cause of Death Revealed" on www.nme.com, an autopsy confirmed that an accidental drug overdose of a mixture of cocaine and the prescription painkiller tramadol was the cause of his death shortly before his thirty-sixth birthday.

Method Man (Clifford Smith, 1971), the youngest member of the Wu-Tang Clan. Method Man is known for his distinctively smooth vocal tracks and was one of the first members of the Clan to release a solo album, *Tical*, which was popular among fans, receiving both critical acclaim and success. He received a Grammy for his song "I'll Be There for You/You're All I Need to Get By" with Mary J. Blige. He has also found success as an actor. He has appeared in both film and television, most notably in the series *The Wire*. He also appeared in the film *How High* and the sitcom *Method & Red*.

Raekwon (Corey Woods, 1970), whose rapping style is unique. His raps are fast-paced rhythmic lyrics spoken poetically in New York slang. The lyrics usually reference the wealth and power gained from illegal drug trades. His successful solo album, *Only Built 4 Cuban Linx…*, is generally considered to be one of the best of the solo albums recorded by any members of the Clan.

Ghostface Killah (Dennis Coles, 1970), who is one of the most consistent and artistically involved members in all the Wu-Tang Clan's albums. His rap style is a highly energized one, and his rhythm is often rather emotional and intense. His critically acclaimed debut album, *Ironman*, brought about resounding success, encouraging him to record twelve more successful solo albums.

Inspectah Deck (Jason Hunter, 1970), who has had a great deal of vocal performances recorded on the Wu-Tang albums, including the fan favorite *Wu-Tang Forever*. His distinct style of rap reflects difficult phrasing and complicated rhyming schemes. Although quite a popular rapper with fans, his attempts with early solo albums *Uncontrolled Substance* and *The Movement* weren't received very well by them. In addition to being a rapper, Inspectah Deck went on to become a successful producer in his own right, providing the beats for rap artists within as well as outside of the Clan family.

U-God (Lamont Hunter, 1970), who has experienced many bouts of incarceration. One of the founding members of the Wu-Tang Clan, he has had very little media exposure and attention. As a result, he has limited vocals on the group's debut album *Enter the Wu-Tang (36 Chambers)*, yet his distinctive low baritone voice can be heard on select tracks.

Masta Killa (Elgin Turner, 1969), who, in the early days of the Wu-Tang Clan, was mentored by GZA. As the only member of the Wu-Tang Clan who was an inexperienced rapper, he spent a great deal of time learning the ropes. He also doesn't appear on many of the tracks in their debut album *Enter the Wu-Tang (36 Chambers)*, due to being incarcerated. However, he is artistically involved with the *Wu-Tang Forever* album, and his tracks are distinctive because of his talk-rap style. He was also the last member to release his own solo album, *No Said Date*.

Not officially regarded as one of the founding members of the Wu-Tang Clan yet friends with many of the Clan's members, Cappadonna (Darryl Hill, 1969) is featured in quite a lot of the Clan's solo music projects. He appeared on Raekwon's hit single "Ice Cream" and also recorded on Ghostface Killah's solo album *Ironman*. His first participation with the Wu-Tang Clan was in 1997 on the album *Wu-Tang Forever*, where he recorded on only a few specific tracks and is credited as a featured artist. His appearances and involvement in the Clan's third album, *The W*, rose significantly, and he was no longer considered just a featured artist. However, due to disagreements with RZA over royalties, Cappadonna doesn't appear as a recording artist on the Wu-Tang Clan's fourth album, *Iron Flag*. Years later, Cappadonna seems to be artistically involved with Wu-Tang again, having performed with the group in its concert "Rock the Bells" and with the appearance of his vocal recordings on their fifth album, *8 Diagrams*.

ARTISTS

Jasper Cropsey

One of the premier painters of the Hudson River School, Jasper Francis Cropsey's works hang in many major museums and the White House. He was born on a little farm in the Rossville section of Staten Island in 1823. His local friends and family called him Frank.

He was a sickly child and used quiet time to teach himself drawing. He showed early promise in architecture when a model house he built took first place at the Mechanic's Institute Fair of 1837. "He was then known locally as the 'boy that built the house,'" according to the Newington-Cropsey Foundation, which keeps his legacy alive.

At fourteen, Frank was already an apprentice architect for the Joseph Trench firm in Manhattan. "While working there, he discovered oil painting and as a teen would go to the National Academy of Design to view the paintings of his idol, Thomas Cole," the foundation states. "At 19, he began to experiment in oil painting, teaching himself after hours in Mr. Trench's office. Soon he had developed to the point that he was exhibited at the National Academy, where his early paintings hung alongside those of Cole, Asher B. Durand, and other early Hudson River School artists. At 21 he was the youngest Associate Member ever elected to the National Academy, and soon left architecture behind (for a while) to concentrate on becoming a full-time landscape painter."

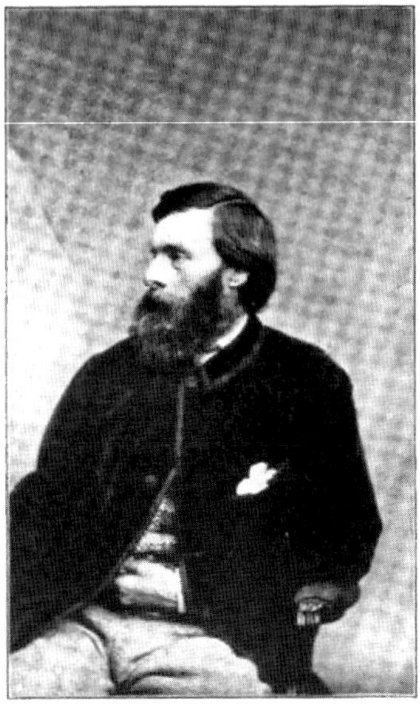

Artist Jasper Cropsey. *Wikimedia Commons.*

Still, his virtuosity with form would aid him in painting some of the most stunning images of the countryside in America and, later, abroad. A master of color known for his rich autumnal landscapes, Cropsey is said to have expressed his spirituality and his patriotism through his canvases, focusing on natural vistas.

Cropsey met the woman who would become his wife, Maria Cooley, in West Milford, New Jersey, and frequently painted scenes from that region throughout his career. Married in 1846, they spent two glorious years in Europe beginning the next year. They focused on Italy, renting an apartment and studio in Rome, but also ventured to France, England, Scotland and Switzerland.

Upon their return to the States in 1849, Cropsey's career took off. He was being paid handsomely for his work, and in 1856, he and his wife returned to Europe, living in London and focusing on England. "His time in England was marked by the completion of *Autumn—On the Hudson River*, his seminal landscape painting now in the National Gallery of Art in Washington, DC, as well as he and Maria being presented to Queen Victoria at St. James Palace in 1861," according to his foundation.

They returned to America in 1863, and Cropsey had the most successful ten years in sales. But the Hudson River School went out of vogue in the latter part of the decade, and the Cropseys would have to sell their beloved Alladin estate in Warwick, New York, and downsize to survive.

In 1885, the Cropseys moved to Hastings on Hudson, where his foundation is based, settling at 49 Washington Avenue, which Cropsey named Ever Rest and which the public can still visit today. The couple lived out the remainder of their lives there, no longer traveling the great distances they did in their youths. His paintings during this period were either local scenes or derived from sketches he'd done previously. He passed away at Ever Rest in 1900 at the age of seventy-seven. His paintings were "rediscovered" and widely celebrated again beginning in the 1960s in America.

LITERARY GREATS

Frank McCourt

The late Pulitzer Prize–winning author Frank McCourt (1930–2009) was first a New York City public teacher for thirty years. "I'm a late bloomer," McCourt told the *New York Times* shortly after publication of *Angela's Ashes* in 1996, when he was sixty-six. His first assignment was at McKee Vocational Technical High School in St. George here.

In a talk at the John F. Kennedy Library in Massachusetts in 2004, McCourt recalled how tough it was in his first Staten Island classes:

> *My first school was a vocational high school on Staten Island. That was the worst thing you could do in those days, go into a vocational high school. I was warned over and over again, "If you're going to teach, stay away from vocational high schools." The movie that came out around that time was called* The Blackboard Jungle *with Glen Ford, and I said, "Oh, Christ, what am I getting myself into?" Fights in the classroom....So, then, I get to this vocational high school in Staten Island. There was a strong Italian population there. But at that time, if you remember* West Side Story, *there were a lot of gang wars going on in New York, and you had these gang wars and these kids coming over. At that time, they used to come up from Brooklyn to Staten Island. So I didn't know how....These kids seemed very mature. The boys were big, and...I didn't tell them. You know, I was very respectful, because some of them....They were on the football team. They could have broken me in two. And the girls—and I was 27 then by the time I got my college degree—and these girls were very mature, these 17 and 18 year olds. I'm afraid that I had lascivious thoughts in my head, and you're not supposed to have that when you're a teacher. And*

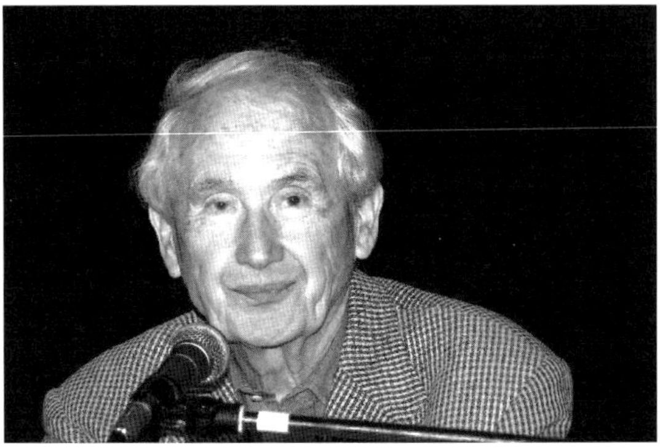

McKee High School teacher Frank McCourt. *PhotoCredit Elke Wetzig.*

> *here I'm facing these monsters, these boys that look like they're gargantuan and the girls were so mature, and I had to adjust to all of that.*

Teaching English was a challenge here, he recalled.

> *Was I going to go in and start teaching English? "No, here's the part of a sentence, the subject, the predicate." No. "Yo, teach! Hey you, he hit me!" And all this stuff is going on, and people are throwing their lunch around the room and, "Can I have a pass? Can I have a pass?" and all that. I developed a whole theory about how do you deal with the pass, and "I've got my period and I've got to go the bathroom. I'm going to need a pass," and, "My mother is dying, I've got to go out to the telephone." "No, you can't!" I wanted to be the stern teacher, in control.*
>
> *No, I was a nincompoop.*

In his follow-up autobiographies, *'Tis* and *Teacher Man*, McCourt wrote a great deal about Staten Island. He wrote in *Teacher Man*, "In the teachers' cafeteria veterans warned me, Son, tell 'em nothing about yourself....You're the teacher. You have a right to privacy. The little buggers are diabolical. They are not, repeat not, your natural friends....You can never get back the bits and pieces of your life that stick in their little heads. Your life, man. It's all you have."

He went on: "The advice was wasted....My life saved my life."

Telling the young people stories from his tragic childhood in Ireland and America kept them engaged and was therapeutic for him, forming the basis for the books he would write when he retired. He would encourage them to write vignettes of their own lives, and they opened up. Surely he had more success with this method later in the very prestigious and competitive

Stuyvesant High School in Manhattan, where many of his students grew to be successful writers themselves, but on Staten Island, he also made a profound connection with young people.

He died on July 19, 2009, in New York City at age seventy-eight. In an interview in the *New York Times* two years before, he said, "I don't want funeral services or memorials. Let them scatter my ashes over the Shannon and pollute the river." Frank McCourt is survived by his wife, Ellen, and his daughter, Maggie, from a previous marriage.

Emily Post

"Etiquette," its chief arbiter Emily Post (1872–1960) once said, "is the science of living. It embraces everything. It is the code of sportsmanship and of honor. It is ethics."

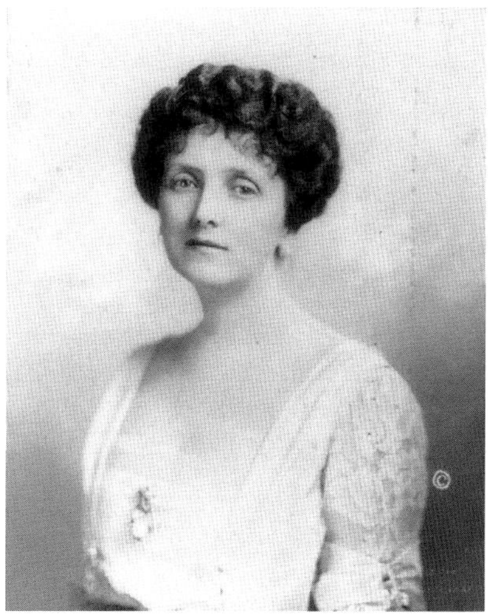

Manners expert Emily Post. *Wikimedia Commons.*

Former debutante Emily Price of Baltimore, Post had been married just a year, fresh from a European honeymoon and pregnant with her first child, when she and her husband, Edwin Main Post, decided to move from Manhattan and Tuxedo Park to quieter shores here in Dongan Hills.

"On Staten Island in 1893, the pace was slower and more relaxed, the expectations not so overwhelming, the afternoon at-homes far fewer—a perfect rhythm for a woman with child," her biographer Laura Claridge wrote in her book *Emily Post: Daughter of the Gilded Age, Mistress of American Manners* in 2009. "In addition, Emily expressed to a few close friends her desire to escape the elaborate entertaining that held New York (Manhattan) and Tuxedo Park in its thrall. That was exhausting for her to contemplate now; she was ambivalent, as well, about sharing her changing shape (however elaborately disguised) her new status as an expectant mother with the people who had nurtured her as their princess. She always disliked being seen at less than her best."

Claridge describes the caravan of horse-drawn vans and local ferries that transported the Posts' furniture from their Manhattan apartment "to their undistinguished but still attractively homey neighborhood. Emily proudly considered herself frugal in light of what she deemed her modest five-bedroom rental, where in addition to her little family, three house servants would live. An attached stable boarded the Posts' three horses and the rooms above their stalls housed a groom and coachman who would double as an odd-job man. On most days a gardener joined the staff as well."

Several of Emily's relatives from Baltimore had moved to Staten Island prior to her coming here.

Though the couple had two sons early in the marriage, it would end in divorce when her husband was blackmailed for adultery. True to form, Post did not make a scene, and they parted civilly. She returned to Manhattan.

According to her *New York Times* obituary, when Post's first widely known book, *Etiquette*, was published in 1922 (when she was fifty years old), "many of the existing handbooks of social usage presupposed wealth and elegance on the part of the reader. Mrs. Post offered advice to society as it was and answered basic problems that confront ordinary people who want to have good manners. Every edition of her book emphasized the basic rule of etiquette: make the other person comfortable. The book was revised ten times and was in its eighty-ninth printing."

In addition to this classic and several other books, Post had a radio show and wrote a daily column, which was still being syndicated to over two hundred newspapers at the time of her death.

And it continues. In April 2017, the *New York Daily News* reviewed the nineteenth edition of *Emily Post's Etiquette* by her great-great-grandchildren Lizzie Post and Daniel Post Senning, saying the over seven-hundred-page volume "stays true to the spirit of her original guides while updating and expanding Post's advice for the modern world." At its heart, the reviewer wrote, "the authors point out, etiquette is about communication and relationships. With the ability to talk to friends instantly via text, or reach thousands on our social media accounts, we should take extra care to communicate respectfully."

For example, the great-great-grandchildren advise, "Treat texting like you would a regular conversation. That means it's probably rude to put off answering a text, or to bombard someone with messages," the review pointed out. "And if you need to break bad news, you should do it with a call or in person, not with a text."

Chapter 9

In Memoriam

September 11, 2001

The commute between Staten Island and Manhattan is an approximately twenty-five-minute ferry ride on the Staten Island Ferry. It provides thousands of Staten Island residents the opportunity to travel for pleasure or work to the most exciting destination in the world. Once the ferry docks in Lower Manhattan, you are a stone's throw away from the city's Financial District, where the World Trade Center was once the heartbeat of this district. Given this ideal commute and the allure of such a powerful city, many Staten Islanders are employed in Manhattan, especially in the Lower Manhattan portion.

The commute to New York City on the Staten Island Ferry (lovingly referred to as "the boat" by Staten Islanders) provides its passengers a quiet moment to sit, devour the day's newspaper, have coffee or catch some last-minute shut-eye before the workday begins. Once the ferry passes Ellis Island and the Statue of Liberty perched in New York Harbor, you instinctively know you're almost on the Manhattan side, and your mind quickly prepares to seize the day and embrace the city's exhilarating adrenaline and power.

September 11, 2001, was a day that shook a nation and especially New York City and its surrounding boroughs to their cores. According to CNN Library's "September 11, 2001: Background and Timeline of the Attacks," 2,753 people perished when hijacked American Airlines Flight 11 and United Airlines Flight 175 were intentionally crashed into the North and South Towers of the World Trade Center in Lower Manhattan. Among those killed, 343 were New York City firefighters, 23 were New York City police

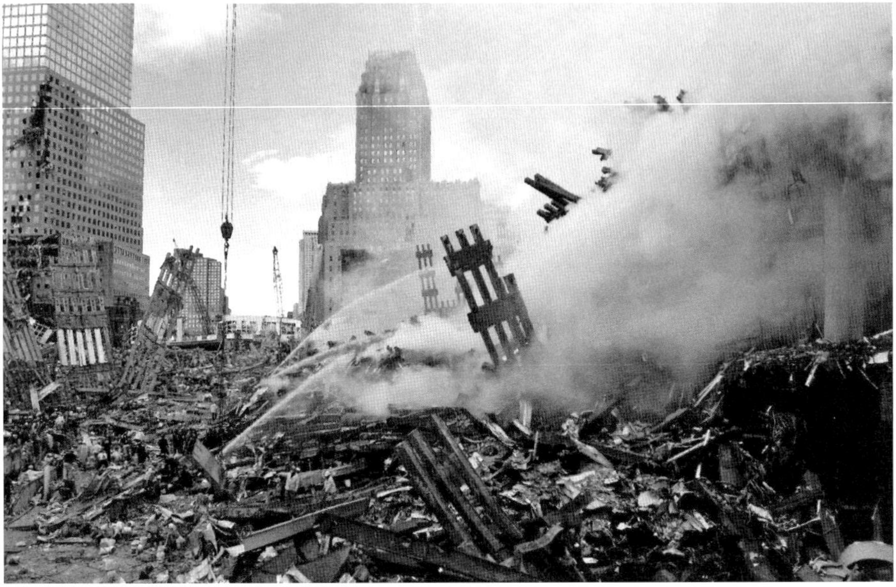

The rubble of the World Trade Center, Ground Zero, Lower Manhattan, two days after the September 11, 2001 terrorist attacks. *Wikimedia Commons.*

officers and 37 were officers of the Port Authority. Furthermore, according to the article "Staten Island's 9/11 Victims: Remembering through Photos and Obituaries" in the *Staten Island Advance*, 275 victims had ties to Staten Island. Their lives and contributions to society will forever be embedded in Staten Island's history.

Every New Yorker has a personal story to tell of that tragic day, and Staten Islanders are no exception. On this fateful day, Lady Liberty, who welcomes all to her beloved New York Harbor, was witness to horrific despair over her beautiful city. Under a billowing cloud of soot and ash, she stood strong and resilient. In those bleakest moments, her silent strength glistened over the dangerous riptides, representing the tenacity and will of the people of the United States, of New York City and of Staten Island. She continues to be a symbol of strength and perseverance to our city and to our great nation.

Those who lost their lives that day were our neighbors, our friends and our loved ones. There are no words to express the depth of pain and sadness, but with such sorrow comes the gifts of unity, solidarity and compassion. Staten Islanders, a community so vastly impacted by this terror attack, banded together to console and comfort one another in our country's darkest hour, displaying a true testament to the resilience of the residents of such an amazing New York City borough.

Today, as the Staten Island Ferry continues to usher residents across the harbor and passes the Statue of Liberty along its route, you are witness to the pride and the freedom she represents, and if you look closely, you see in her eyes a beacon of hope for peace and prosperity.

These pages serve as a tribute to all the Staten Island residents who perished on September 11, 2001. To all the innocent victims and the first responders who put their lives second to save another: may you rest in peace, and may their legacies live on in our hearts and minds. To all community leaders, emergency services, medical providers and New York's Finest and New York's Bravest, thank you.

Terrance Aiken
Peggy Jezycki Alario
Jacquelyn Aldridge-Frederick
Christopher Amoroso
Laura Angilletta
Faustino Apostol
Frank Thomas Aquilino
Louis Arena
Adam P. Arias
Gregg Atlas
Louis Aversano
John Badagliacca
Jane Ellen Baeszler
Katherine Bantis
Walter Baran
Gerard Barbara
Paul V. Barbaro
Arthur Barry
Diane Barry
Carlton Bartels
Michael E. Beekman
Denise Benedetto
John Bergin
Paul Beyer
Brian Bilcher
Carl Bini
Susan Bochino
Mary Boffa
Shawn Bowman
Alfred Braca
Sandra Brace
Greg Buck
Kathleen Burns
Milton Bustillo
Patrick D. Byrne
Lillian Caceres
Salvatore Calabro
Philip V. Calcagno
Michael Cammarata
Vincent Anthony Cangelosi
Lisa Cannava
Brian Cannizzaro
Louis Caporicci
Mark Carney
Peter J. Carroll
Thomas Celic
John Chipura
Steven Chucknick
Frances Ann Cilente
Michael Clarke
Anthony Coladonato
Susan Clancy Conlon

John Connolly
Robert Cordice
Ruben Correa
Francisco Cruz
Kenneth Cubas
Thomas Cullen
Robert Curatolo
Laurence Curia
Beverly Curry
Thomas Damaskinos
Edward D'Atri
Michael D'Auria
Scott Davidson
Edward Day
James DeBlase
Jason DeFazio
Azucena Maria de la Torre
Vito DeLeo
Michael DeRienzo
David DeRubbio
Edward DeSimone
Michael D'Esposito
John DiFato
Carl DiFranco
Donald DiFranco
Debra Ann DiMartino
Stephen Dimino
George DiPasquale
Joseph Di Pilato
Neil Dollard
Joseph Doyle
Felicia Dunn-Jones
Martin J. Egan Jr.
Carole Eggert
Francis Esposito
Lieutenant Michael Esposito
Barbara Etzold
Joseph Farrelly
Rosa Maria Feliciano
David F. Ferrugio
Louis Fersini
Michael Fiore
Stephen J. Fiorelli
John Fischer
Thomas J. Fisher
Sal Fiumefreddo
David Fodor
Michael Fodor
David Fontana
Donald Foreman
Claudia Foster
Peter Freund
Clement Fumando
Deanna Galante
Grace Galante
Cesar Garcia
Gary Geidel
James Giberson
Jeffrey Giordano
John Giordano
Martin Giovinazzo
Monica Goldstein
James Gray
Joseph F. Grillo
Joseph Grzelak
Joseph Gullickson
Barbara Habib
Philip Haentzler
Steven Hagis
Sean S. Hanley
Thomas Hannafin
Vassili Haramis
Frances Haros
Lieutenant Harvey Harrell
Stephen Harrell
Brian Hennessey
Michelle Henrique
Mary Herencia

Jonathan Hohmann
Steven Howell
Steven Huczko
Abid Hussain
Joseph Ianelli
Charles Kasper
Paul Keating
Richard Kelly
Thomas Kelly
Robert Kennedy
Howard Kirschbaum
Stephen Knapp
Shekhar Kumar
Kenneth Kumpel
Patricia Anne Kuras
James Ladley
David LaForge
Vincent Laieta
Robert Lane
Mary Lou Langley
Michele Lanza
Stephen Lauria
Jeannine LaVerde
James Leahy
Firefighter Neil J. Leavy
Lorraine Lee
Daniel Libretti
Vincent M. Litto
Lee Ludwig
Marie Lukas
Linda Luzzicone
Robert H. Lynch
Joseph Maffeo
Charles Margiotta
Paul Martini
Anne Martino-Cramer
Joseph A. Mascali
Michael Massaroli
Robert Mattson
Walter Matuza Jr.
Charles J. Mauro
Charles A. Mauro Jr.
John McAvoy
Lieutenant William McGinn
Scott McGovern
Stephanie McKenna
Timothy McSweeney
William Micciulli
Philip D. Miller
Benjamin Millman
Louis Minervino
Paul Mitchell
Richard Miuccio
Louis Modafferi
Carl Molinaro
Kristen Montanaro
Christopher Mozzillo
Peter Mulligan
Richard Myhre
Mario Nardone
Troy Nilsen
Brian Nunez
Philip P. Ognibene
Joseph Ogren
William O'Keefe
Linda Oliva
Edward Oliver
Eric Olsen
Jeffrey Olsen
Steven Olson
Pablo Ortiz
Jeffrey Palazzo
Alan Palumbo
Paul Pansini
Salvatore Papasso
Cira Patti
Carl Peralta
Glenn Perry

Danny Pesce
Mark Petrocelli
Philip Petti
Nicholas Pietrunti
Susan Ancona Pinto
Joseph Plumitallo
Wanda Prince
Edward Pullis
Patricia Puma
Michael Quilty
Leonard J. Ragaglia
Eugene Raggio
Laura Marie Ragonese-Snik
Peter Raimondi
Michelle Reed
Joseph Reina
Karen Renda
Anthony Rodriguez
Keith Roma
Lloyd Rosenberg
Nicholas Rossomando
Thomas Sabella
Joseph Sacerdote
Brock Safronoff
John Santore
John Schardt
Angela Scheinberg
Adriane Scibetta
Adele Sessa
Thomas Sgroi
Robert Shay
Stephen Siller
Paul Simon
Marianne Simone
Rosemary Smith
Sushil Solanki
Thomas Sparacio
Frank Spinelli
Michael Stabile
Richard Stadelberger
Anthony Starita
Jeffrey Stark
Alexander Steinman
Larry Sumaya
Harry Taback
Joann Tabeek
John Talignani
Maurita Tam
Allan Tarasiewicz
Darryl Taylor
Anthony Tempesta
John Tierney
Lisa Spina Trerotola
Jennifer Lynn Tzemis
Kenneth Van Auken
Azael Vasquez
Francine Virgilio
Joseph Visciano
Barbara Walsh
Jeffrey Walz
Kenneth White
Mark Whitford
Patrick Woods
Myrna Yaskulka
Olabisi Layeni Yee
Jacqueline Young
Edwin Zambrana Jr.

All names were published in the *Staten Island Advance* article "Staten Island's 9/11 Victims: Remembering through Photos and Obituaries."

Selected Bibliography

Alice Austen Museum. AliceAusten.org.

American Museum of Natural History. Anthropological Papers of the American Museum of Natural History, Vols. 3–4.

Andre, John. *Major Andre's Journal.* Tarrytown, NY: W. Abbatt, 1930.

Asbury, Edith Evans. "Jacqueline Onassis Goes to Snug Harbor." *New York Times*, 1976.

Atlas Obscura. "Kreischer Mansion." 2017. obscura.com.

Barry, Gerald J. *The Sailors' Snug Harbor: A History, 1801–2001.* New York: Fordham University Press, 2000.

Beacham, Kevin. "Time Travelin with the Genius." 2005. grandgood.com.

Beagle, Ryan. "Top 5 Rappers from Staten Island." 2016. hiphopgoldenage.com.

Bowery Boys History. "Snug Harbor: A Port in the Storm." 2007. boweryboyshistory.com.

Brown, Chip. "Escape from New York." *New York Times*, 1994.

Buckley, Cara. "Bohemia by the Bay." *New York Times*, 2007.

Canby, Henry Seidel. *Thoreau.* Boston: Houghton Mifflin, 1939.

Cares, Kathryn. "Log-Cabin Retreat Once Stood on Emerson Hill." *Staten Island Advance*, 2007.

Census Bureau. Richmond County (Staten Island Borough), New York. "Staten Island." State & QuickFacts. census.gov.

Chan, Sewell. "That Old Tale About S.I.? Hold on Now." *New York Times*, 2007.

Cheslow, Jerry. "If You're Thinking of Living in: Grymes Hill." *New York Times*, 1989.
Clark, Marcia. *Without a Doubt*. New York: Viking Press, 1997.
Clough, Shepard. *A History of the Western World.* Lexington, MA, 1969.
CNN Library. "September 11 2001: Background and Timeline of the Attacks." N.d.
Cody, Buffalo Bill. *Story of the Wild West and Camp-fire Chats*. Vol. 3. N.p.: Historical Publishing, 1888.
The Conference House Association. ConferenceHouse.org.
Connelly, James C. "How New York Acquired Staten Island." Proceedings of the New Jersey Historical Society 8, no. 4, New Series (1923).
Dunlap, David. "Dispute Grows." *New York Times*, 1987.
Eckel, Peter J. "Father Christopher C. Drumgoole, Shepherd of the Homeless Newsboys." HistoryReference.org. History Reference.
Ellis, Edward Robb. *The Epic of New York City*. N.p.: Old Town Books, 1966.
Encyclopedia Britannica. 11th ed. "Staten Island." New York, 1910.
Fitzpatrick, Mallick. "John C. Drumgoole." *The Catholic Encyclopedia*. Vol 5. New York: Robert Appleton Company, 1909.
Fowler, Will. *Santa Anna of Mexico.* N.p.: Bison Books, 2009.
Freighery, Kate. "Robert Richard Randall and Sailors' Snug Harbor." Greenwich Village History, 2011. GreenwichvillageHistory.wordpress.com.
Fressola, Michael. "'Landmarks' on Staten Island: 11th Hour Triumph of History or Destruction by Development?" *Staten Island Advance*, 2015.
Garibaldi, Giuseppe. *Autobiography*. N.p., 1889.
Garibaldi-Meucci Museum. "History of the House."
"Globe Telephone Company 1884—Famous ATT Patent Fight." 1996–2007. scripophily.com. worldwideinvention.com.
Greene, Evarts B., and Virginia D. Harrington. *American Population Before the Federal Census of 1790*. New York: Syracuse University Press, 1932.
Haunted Staten Island. HauntedStatenIsland.com.
Hine, Charles Gilbert. *History and Legend of Howard Avenue and the Serpentine Road, Grymes Hill, Staten Island*. New York: Hine Brothers, 1914.
Hine, Charles Gilbert, and William T. Davis, *Legends, Stories and Folklore of Old Staten Island.* N.p.: Staten Island Historical Society, 1925.
Historic House Trust of New York City. HistoricHouseTrust.org.
Historic Richmond Town. HistoricRichmondTown.org.
Hobbs, Linda. "Vbeat: Clan in Da Front." *Vibe*, 2007.
Irving, Washington. *The Sketch Book of Geoffrey Crayon, Gent*. N.p., 1819 and 1820.

Italian Society of Electrotechnics. aei.it.

Jackson, K.T., ed. *Encyclopedia of New York*. New Haven, CT: Yale University Press, 1995.

Jacobson, Jerome. "Burial Ridge, Tottenville, Staten Island, N.Y.: Archaeology at New York City's Largest Prehistoric Cemetery." Staten Island Institute of Arts and Sciences, 1980.

Keister, Douglas. *Stories in Stone New York: A Field Guide to New York City Area Cemeteries and Their Residents*. N.p.: Gibbs Smith, 2011.

Khoudari, Amy. *Looking in the Shadows: The Life of Alice Austen*. N.p.: iuniverse, 2006.

Kroessler, Jeffrey. *New York Year by Year: A Chronology of the Great Metropolis*. New York: New York University Press, 2002.

Kugel, Seth. "Staten Island: Getting Beyond the Ferry." *New York Times*, 2008.

Lehto, Steve. *American Murder Houses: A Coast to Coast Tour of the Most Notorious Houses of Homicide*. New York: Penguin, 2016.

Linedecker, Clifford. *Marcia Clark: Her Private Trials and Public Triumphs*. N.p.: Pinnacle Publishing Company, n.d.

Lore, Diane C. "Staten Island's Kreischer Mansion Up for Sale for $9.5 Million." *Staten Island Advance*, 2016.

Love, Shayla. "Inside Seguine Mansion, Staten Island's Eccentric Historic House." gothamist.com, 2014.

Meucci, Sandra. *Antonio and the Electric Scream: The Man Who Invented the Telephone*. Boston: Branden Books, 2010.

Mission of the Immaculate Virgin. "A Brief History of MIV." 2009. mountloretto.org.

Morgan, Susan. *Bombay Anna: The Real Story and Remarkable Adventures of the* King and I *Governess*. Berkeley: University of California Press, 2008.

National Park Service. nps.gov.

National Register of Historic Places. www.nationalregisterofhistoricplaces.com.

National Trust for Historic Preservation. savingplaces.org.

New York City Department of Parks and Recreation. "Conference House Park." NYCGovparks.org.

New York City Landmarks Preservation Commission. "William T. and Mary Marcellite Garner Mansion." 2011.

New York Public Library. "New York City: Staten Island on the Web." 2013.

New York Sun. "A Home for Ancient Mariners." 2007.

New York Times. "A Bill for the Preservation of the Historic Mansion. Continental Congress Committee There Rejected Lord Howe's Offer of Amnesty." 1901.

———. "Father Drumgoole Honored." 1894.
———. "Italian Commission to Honor Garibaldi." 1917.
———. "Italians Dedicate Garibaldi Memorial." 1907.
———. "Old Friends Honor Miss Alice Austen, Photographer for 50 Years Has Her Day." 1951.
NME.com. "Ol Dirty Bastard—Cause of Death Revealed." 2004.
Noble Maritime Collection. noblemaritime.org.
NYFaithInformation.org. "Saints of New York: Father John C. Drumgoole (1816–1888)." 2015.
Rashbaum, William K. "Grisly Mob Killing at S.I. Mansion Is Detailed." *New York Times*, 2006.
Readers' Digest. "The Story of Charles Goodyear." January 1958.
Realty Co. "City Will Preserve Old Billop House. Landmark at Tottenville, S.I., Was Scene of Peace Conference in '76." *New York Times*, 1926.
Salmon, Patricia. "Staten Island Memories: The Business of Brewing." *Staten Island Advance*, 2012.
Sanderson, Eric. *Mannahatta: A Natural History of New York City*. New York: Harry N. Abrams, 2009.
Schellmann, Hilke. "Spirits Moving on S.I." *Wall Street Journal*, 2012.
Scheltema, Gajus, and Helen Westerhuijs. *Exploring Historic Dutch New York*. New York: Dover Publications, 2011.
Seguine Mansion. seguinemansion.org.
Shorto, Russell. *The Island at the Center of the World: The Epic Story of Dutch Manhattan and the Forgotten Colony that Shaped America*. 1st ed. New York City: Vintage Books, 2004.
Sietsema, Robert. "Killmeyer's and the Kreischer Mansion: Meat and Murder on Staten Island." *Village Voice*, 2010.
Simcoe, John Graves. *A History of the Operations of a Partisan Corps Called the Queen's Rangers*. Exeter, UK, 1787.
Smithsonian Affiliations. 2016. affiliations.si.edu.
Snug Harbor Cultural Center and Garden. snug-harbor.org.
The Source. rocklistmusic.co.uk.
Staten Island Advance. "Staten Island's 9/11 Victims: Remembering Through Photos and Obituaries." N.d.
Staten Island Institute of Arts and Sciences. ny.com.
Staten Island Museum. StatenIslandmuseum.org.
Trevelyan, G.M. *Garibaldi's Defense of the Roman Republic*. London: Longmans, 1907.

United States House of Representatives. House Resolution 269. 2002.
White, N., and E. Willensky. *AIA Guide to New York City*. 4th ed. N.p.: Three Rivers Press, 2000.
Wilson, Claire. "Developed Enough as It Is, Thanks." *New York Times*, 2006.
———. "Rosebank, Staten Island: A Quiet Slice of New York Waterfront." *New York Times*, 2006.

About the Authors

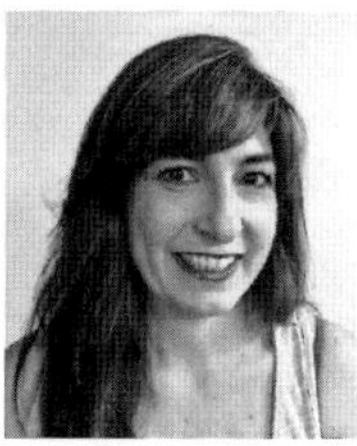

Theresa Anarumo, a native Staten Islander, is a former New York Radio Broadcast account executive and elementary school educator. She currently resides in Manhattan with her husband, son and lovable dachshund, Tiffany.

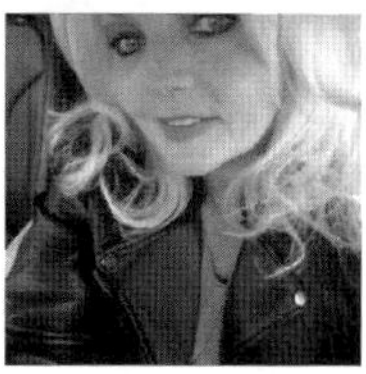

Maureen Seaberg is the author of *Struck by Genius* (HMH, 2014) and has written for the *New York Times*; *Vogue*; *O, the Oprah magazine*; and many other publications. She is also an expert blogger on the senses for *Psychology Today*. A native Staten Islander, she lives on Ward Hill.